A Perfect Love

And a Blessed Life

As Told by Joe Frisinger

And Written by Lynn Thompson

They were married for 54 years.
During those years they never said
a harsh word to the other and they
never had an argument.
They regarded each other as the most
Wonderful person in the World.
They truly had
A Perfect Love And a Blessed Life.

DEDICATION

TO MY DEAR WIFE, JANE

AND TO HER PARENTS,

EDWARD AND MARGARET SCANLON

CONTENTS

ACKNOWLEDGMENTS

I would first like to acknowledge and thank LYNN THOMPSON for the outstanding job she has done in writing this book, which is my tribute to my wife, Jane, in *A PERFECT LOVE and A BLESSED LIFE*. Lynn is a joy to work with and her experience in both writing and interviewing made the creation of this book possible.

I would also like to acknowledge and thank the three wonderful live-in caregivers who blessed Jane and me with their presence. Each of them did an outstanding job in providing care to Jane. Our first live-in caregiver was ROSE TAUHELANGI, our second was KIMBERLY SHEPHERD, and our third was MARIAH STYS. I thank each of them with all my heart.

I want to acknowledge and thank friends Gary and Ellen Rexrode, who, when Jane first fell, came over to help me care for Jane for the following ten days. They provided both help and emotional support to Jane and to me as well, until a great couple from Michigan came to help.

I want to acknowledge and thank wonderful friends Freddie and Sharon DeCoopman who cut short their vacation in Florida to first drive home to Michigan and then fly out to stay with us and help care for Jane.

I want to acknowledge and thank great friends Doug, Marge and daughter Melanie Shortall from Rhode Island who have become like family. They have visited Jane's grave at least eight times and have placed flowers on her grave. They have also helped me when I have gone back to Rhode Island.

Finally, I want to acknowledge and thank the staff of CREATE SPACE for the professional help they have provided in the creation of this book.

1. INTRODUCTION

You are going to be reading a love story. This is a story about a deep love between two ordinary people. A love so strong it was never meant to be broken.

It is about a marriage of over 54 years during which there was never a harsh word between the two of us nor was there ever a single argument. Both Jane and I respected and admired each other so much and we had a great need to be with each other always. At night, the last words we each heard were "I love you!"

We felt so very blessed to be married to each other and we never wanted to be apart. Being together we both felt so happy and so confident. We were equals, focused on the needs of the other. Each of us felt that the other was the most wonderful person on earth.

The story begins as I first meet Jane and how our meeting came about. Later – in the way of background – is a telling of our childhoods and the challenges we faced and how bravely and unselfishly Jane faced the challenge of being the family bread winner for her mother and herself.

You will also see mentions of a Guardian Angel. Jane and I are both Catholic and we would go to Mass every Sunday, including the Sunday before she died. Jane's beliefs were deeper than mine. While I believe many things that are in the Bible, I also have many doubts – such as, I believe in evolution rather than creation. But I am absolutely positive that I have a Guardian Angel, who guided me to Jane and has also saved my life six times and in one case, saved the lives of five others, including Jane. You will read about such cases later.

Everyone has needs and throughout our lives we are constantly encountering options. We consciously or unconsciously make choices. A perfect marriage is not achieved by luck. It is achieved by reaching common goals and making life choices that support those common goals. This book is about how we achieved our "perfect marriage" of 54 years.

2. THE BEGINNING

It is 8pm on Wednesday and I have been studying for the last three hours and I will study for another three hours before going to bed.

I am a young Naval officer who is attached to the Naval Assault Group stationed in Little Creek, Virginia. I am currently attending the Naval Justice School in Newport, Rhode Island and I am in my fifth week of an eight-week program.

As a member of the Assault Group, we are frequently deployed and we feel that we are exempt from having, as one of our collateral duties, the assignment of serving as defense council or as prosecutor in a Captain's military hearing. Naval Personnel thought otherwise. We were not exempt and I was selected to attend the Naval Justice School in Newport.

I might mention that the Assault Group was an elite Naval Force that included as members both former Senator Robert Kerry from Nebraska and former Senator John Kerry (now US Secretary of State) from Massachusetts, along with the son of General Westmoreland, who was a graduate of the Naval Academy.

The Naval Assault Group (now called Naval Special Warfare) suffered very high casualties in Korea. Even though we were line officers serving as Officer of the Deck aboard ship while going to missions, there was the feeling that – with our high casualty rate – those who volunteered might not be – as the Irish would kindly say – "the sharpest knife in the drawer."

While many other officers in the school were clearly much smarter than me, I was determined – by studying twice as long – to not let the Assault Group down. During the first four weeks I never left the base and after seven hours of class, I would study six hours and on weekends I would study twelve to fourteen hours. I even purchased the first year Harvard Law books. At the end of each week there would a class standing list posted. At the end of the fourth week I was number 2 out of a class of 48. This was Not to Last.

That Wednesday evening I was in my room studying. At 8pm my Guardian Angel said (in my head), "Go to the Mooring and go now!" I know this sounds strange, but it is true. My Guardian Angel had already saved my life two times – and in the coming years would save it another four times – so when I heard that voice, I listened. I put my book down, took off my uniform, put on civilian clothes and drove down to the very popular

Mooring Restaurant located waterside in Newport. When I arrived at the Mooring, I looked at a table that had five beautiful girls and among the five was Jane Scanlon.

I knew instantly why my Guardian Angel told me to go to the Mooring, as when I looked at Jane I realized that I was already in love with her – and I felt that I had been in love with her all my life. What a glorious feeling. As it turned out, the five girls were Telephone Operators. Luckily one of them was an operator whom I knew, as she worked on the satellite facility base and I would see her (Ellen Moriarty) when I made a weekly call to my parents. I was standing by a post near their table, and Ellen said, "Joe, that post will stand without you. Come and sit down."

And that is how this love story begins. As the girls were leaving, I asked Jane if I could see her. She agreed that I could pick her up at work the next day and we would take the beautiful Ocean Drive together and talk and I would have her home before her dinner time.

Our first real date was on a Saturday and we went up to Boston to see the movie *Around the World in 80 Days*.

Little did we know then that when we got married, our first home – for almost two years – would be a tiny villa in Naples with vineyards on one side and a farm house and barn on the other side. While tiny, it had a balcony that overlooked the entire bay of Naples and the island of Capri. Nothing could be more romantic.

And, regarding my standing in class, it did not last and I finished just barely in the top half in the group's standing. So, I did not make the Assault Group proud, but ending up in the top half, I did not let them down. As I left the school I had found the future – my precious Jane – and I was the happiest person in the world.

During my marriage with Jane, it was no longer "me" it was – joyfully – "us" and that is covered in this book.

3. OUR WEDDING AND HONEYMOON

When I met Jane, for me it was love at first sight. But in the Assault Group, we were almost constantly deployed, and I knew that was not a way to start a marriage. After three years in the Assault Group, I was selected to serve on the staff of Admiral Brown (NATO Supreme Commander Allied Forces Southern Europe) in Naples, Italy, which was considered to be the best duty one could attain in the Navy.

Having achieved shore duty, I was able to ask Jane if she would marry me, and I did so in writing. A copy of my letter to Jane is part of this book. Luckily, her response was "Yes" and our wedding was planned for Saturday, April 23, 1960.

Jane, with the help of her friend Ellen Moriarty, planned a beautiful wedding. The wedding took place at Saint Lucy's church in nearby Middletown (a small town adjoining Newport). Jane looked stunning in her wedding dress and the ceremony was very formal, which perhaps is another word for traditional. The reception was held at the Newport Navy Officer's Club which overlooks Newport Harbor. The weather was sunny and the church was filled with flowers. Everything went perfectly. Jane and I thanked everyone there who was in attendance. We especially thanked Jane's mother, my parents, and the members of the Wedding Party. Together, Jane and I cut the wedding cake. I still have a small piece of our wedding cake, carefully wrapped, kept in a dresser drawer. A very beautiful wedding and reception.

Following the reception, my parents drove us to the train station and we took the train to Boston. On Sunday morning we went to 8am Mass and then flew to Bermuda to begin our honeymoon. In Bermuda we stayed at the very romantic Four Ways Inn. For tourists in Bermuda, travel is either by walking, by bus, or by moped. We chose to travel by mopeds – but as I watched Jane taking a short ride alongside an instructor on a moped next to her – I suddenly became very, very concerned about her safety. What a wonderful relief it was when I saw her come back safely.

Both Jane and I love the sea and after breakfast on Monday we went on a charter sailboat for a lovely sail around Bermuda's many islands. On the following days we enjoyed the beaches and enjoyed riding our mopeds.

On Thursday our airline called and asked if we could fly out a few days later than scheduled, as they were over-booked with many residents of the various British Islands flying to London to attend Princess Margaret's wedding to Anthony Armstrong Jones at Westminster Abbey. The airline said that they would pay for our room at the Inn plus a daily meal allowance.

We quickly agreed. We also remembered the story told about Mark Twain's visit to Bermuda. Apparently when he was talking with a Church of England priest, Twain remarked, "Bermuda is so beautiful it must be like heaven." The priest, perhaps considering Mark Twain's rather colorful life, is said to have replied, "Well, enjoy it then, while you can." We continued to enjoy it for two more days.

Leaving Bermuda, we continued our honeymoon by flying to London. We stayed in central London for two days and then drove to Devon where we stayed in Bed & Breakfast homes in small villages. Upon returning to London, we barely got there in time to make our plane to Naples. In fact, our plane was already on the runway and they had a car drive us out to it. My diplomatic status, which some NATO officers received, must have helped. We then got on a plane to Naples, Italy, where our wonderful little villa awaited us.

A new home and the beginning of a new life.

4. OUR WONDERFUL TINY HOME IN NAPLES

Two months before our wedding, I had asked Jane if she wanted to live with the Italians or in apartments that contained mostly Americans, and she said, "The Italians." That was perfect because it was also what I wanted but I wanted her to make the choice.

In the northern part of Naples there were hundreds of very beautiful homes, some large, some small. So I would go out in the early evening and knock on doors, and ask, "Villa si loca?" The answer was always "No!" In some cases, "This has been our home for over 500 years!" And some would say, "No, but come in for a glass of wine." Which I would do, and I enjoyed. Finally, I discovered this tiny road with the name Disceso Giola ("little road going down"). This road was built at the same time as the Appian Way with the same blocks and the same width. Along this very curvy street there was a total of 13 homes and at the bottom was a summer home of one of the Caesars. The home was still there and was lived in by a Marquess (a title of nobility – the eldest son of a Duke).

There is a turn at the bottom of the road where there's a tiny little harbor, which is the very spot where Naples was founded 3,000 years ago by the Greeks. When we were there it was also a very popular spot for smugglers coming in with such things as cigarettes. The harbor had three rather large brick buildings that were probably a few hundred years old. They were all attached and they contained three families.

As I went down this road, there was this very small two-story home that looked like it was built in the 1930s. One unit was on the ground floor, with the second unit upstairs. Each had two bedrooms, a tiny bathroom, a larger open room and a tiny kitchen that only one person could be in at a time, it was that small. I knocked on the door of the upper unit, and was answered by an American, who said they were leaving in another three weeks and gave me the name of the owner who was a doctor in Rome, who also had a beautiful home on the island of Capri.

I called the doctor and luckily, he spoke perfect English. I said I would love to rent the house, and that I would paint either the outside or the inside of the house, whichever he chose for me to do. It was still five weeks away before I was flying back to marry Jane. He said, "Paint the outside of the house." So I immediately started. I would get up extremely early, 4:30am, well before the sun came up. Luckily there was not heavy rain at that time, in late March. I had the house painted white as it had been originally, and

I completed it in ten days. He did have the inside painted as soon as the couple moved out. I then was able to purchase a bed from the military PX (general supply store for military with identification). The bed was from Denmark, and I was also able to purchase a chest. Both were teak. Later I purchased a second full-size bed for the other bedroom. Across the road from this villa was a farmhouse with a barn. In the barn they had some furniture. The farmer by the name of Strata brought over a chest and also a few chairs.

The next Saturday I drove up to Rome and went to a beautiful furniture store on Via Condotti which is the most famous shopping street in all of Rome. The street ends at the famous Spanish steps. I had previously purchased an engagement ring for Jane and our wedding rings at Bulgari's, which is one of the four most famous jewelry stores in the world. Near Bulgari's is this very elegant furniture store. I went in to the furniture store and I ordered a beautiful dining room table with six chairs, which we still have in our home in Princeville on Kauai. They asked, "When do you want it to be delivered?" In answering that question, I thought, well, we will be landing in Naples on May 6 on our flight from London which is arriving at 11am in the morning. Getting the car and then going to our Villa would be about a 40-minute drive. So I asked if they could bring it down at 1:30pm on that same day. They said, "Certainly."

When I mentioned this to people on the NATO base, they all without exception said, "Are you kidding? You are going to be lucky to get it within a week of that date!" They did not know how wonderful this particular store was, and how I trusted them! We did land at 11am. We did get our Volkswagen. And we got to our villa before noon. Jane was absolutely amazed at the beauty of the location and the views. It was like being in the country while we were actually in a big city.

Promptly at 1:25pm we heard a truck coming down the road. The truck pulled in to our driveway at exactly 1:30pm, and our dining room table and chairs were delivered, right on time.

Around our villa was a wall which was very common in Italy. The lower unit of the villa did not have a view. In our top unit we had a balcony which was forty feet long and approximately four feet wide. We had a view of the entire bay of Naples. To Jane and me it was heaven on earth. We were so happy. Jane could almost not believe the view and location. Our tiny Naples villa was in a magical spot. What a marvelous way to begin a marriage. It was a time of great joy for us.

We also discovered, thanks to the farmer across the road, that there is a cave up the road that was and had been the local winery for the last 2,000 years. And it was still there. He explained that you go up with your liter containers, and you get either white (blanc) or red (rouge) wine, straight from the cask. French have this wonderful saying, *"In water one sees one's own face but in wine one beholds the heart of another."* A romantic saying.

Our first purchase together was a 12-foot Lug Rig wooden sailboat, for $175. This is a simple boat to handle and is a very seaworthy small boat. This particular boat was an Olympic class in the late 1800s. It was very inexpensive and yet exactly what we wanted. We sailed this little boat every Saturday and during the summer we might sail it one day during the week when the days were long. We loved sailing and Jane became a wonderful sailor. We will talk more about her sailing experiences later.

5. OUR LIFE IN ITALY

Jane and I felt so lucky and blessed to have our married life begin in this beautiful setting of Naples. Each day we marveled at the fact that we were indeed here and that 2,000 years ago a Roman Caesar had come down our road many times to go to his summer home and that on the little cove just off the bottom of the road was where Naples was founded. We were not only surrounded by beauty, we were also surrounded by history and that is so amazing.

We were thankful each day for the two of us being together where we were. Caesar also had a tunnel built through the hill and that was still open and showed no damage. In fact during World War Two, the residents on one side of the tunnel would come into the tunnel for their safety when American planes were bombing the industrial plants on the other side of the tunnel. Now, the tunnel provided me a quick way to go by bicycle to the NATO headquarters only three miles away. I would do that sometimes so Jane could use the car – our Volkswagen – to go shopping.

Jane and I would often drive up to Rome and attend Mass in St. Peters. Pope John the Twenty-third was very much a Pope of the people and he was very liberal and very popular. Jane and I felt that he was great. We would then tour a small area of the city of Rome – learning a little bit about Rome on each trip as we wanted to know the history of Rome for when we would take visitors to Rome as part of our visit together. There is a USO (United Services Organizations) building only two blocks away from the Vatican and we would stop there to use the restrooms and get a light snack. On other weekends we would drive down to Sorrento, on the opposite side of the Bay of Naples, and then take the scenic Amalfi Drive to the beautiful village of Positano where we would have lunch. About every six weeks we would take a ferry to the island of Capri and spend the day there. From the ferry landing we would take the funicular up to the town of Capri and take some walks there. Then we would ride a bus (a very short trip) up to Anacapri where we would first visit the Villa San Michele and then we would take the chairlift to the top of the island. From there we would go back to the ferry landing and take a ferry back to Naples; a very enjoyable outing in a day.

Here it is important to point out that we tried to sail our 12-foot boat over to Capri a total of five times. Each time we made it more than half-way and then the winds would stop and we would just be floating in the middle of the bay until mid-afternoon when the winds would return and, having no money to stay overnight in expensive Capri, we would head back home.

As newlyweds we were very proud of our dining room table and we often had people over for wine and cheese, a tradition we continued all of our married life. We were also blessed to have relatives visit us. Jane's beloved brother Robert and sister-in-law Kay visited us and we were happy to show them both Rome and then the Amalfi Coast. When my parents came to visit, they made a stop to visit us in Paris first because they had not been to Paris before. They had made arrangements to stay at George V Hotel, one of the most famous 5-Star hotels in the world. We had arrived the previous day and found they had central heat. We did not have heat in our home, apart from a kerosene heater for our bathroom in the morning. So we did not fully appreciate the luxuriousness of the hotel, being unused to so much heat, and it was the only time in our life that we stayed at a 5-Star hotel.

We were at the airport when my parents' flight came in and this was one of the few times I was able to impress my parents. With diplomatic status, I was able to walk them right through customs, which I did. We stayed in Paris just a few days. My father took us to the top of the Eiffel tower for dinner one evening. They returned with us to Naples and they also enjoyed the beauty of the views from our villa and joined us for wine and dinner each evening, which Jane had planned and prepared in advance. It was wonderful to have them visit. One of my uncles and his wife (Max and Elizabeth Frisinger) also came to visit us. The Frisinger family business was building highways and runways throughout the mid-west. Being familiar with highway construction – as were all six sons of my grandfather – Max was very impressed with the Amalfi Drive, full of twisting turns and dramatic drops to the ocean on the right hand side. He thought it was almost miraculous that they could build this road in such rugged conditions. Additionally, we also had a couple of Jane's friends from Newport come into port on a cruise ship and spend the day with us on their way to Greece.

When I first met Jane, I knew that she was the one I had loved since I was born. When we were married, we were both deeply in love with each other, yet during the first four to five months of our marriage, our love became more and more intense. After five months of marriage we had a long talk one night, and we described the intensity of our love. We vowed that we never wanted to be apart, not even for a day. We both regarded the other person as the most wonderful person in the world. As a result, no Navy career for me, for as a line officer, in order to have the very slim possibility of reaching flag rank, I would have to be at sea for the next nine years. We also did not want to have a job where I had to travel. This decision still made a lot of jobs available to us. I could work for a city, I could work for a hospital, I could work for a university, so there were still many possibilities that would allow us to be home with each other every night. And we felt so happy after making this decision, and thought, "This is a wonderful life we are going to have together."

While living there in Naples, I had already built up a number of vacation days. During the following year we took three vacation trips, touring southern Europe, going as far north as Paris, but spending more time in Northern Italy, Bavaria (part of Germany) and Switzerland. We would always stay in B&B (Bed & Breakfast) homes. Sometimes it would be so delightful, for example at a farmer's home, when the whole family would come out after breakfast to wave us good-bye. We enjoyed the people and the adventure – we felt we became part of the community. The people of the homes where we stayed could see how happy the two of us were together, and so they responded to that.

After our fifth month of marriage we learned that Jane was expecting our first child, due in late May or early June. We were so happy about this, and we knew each of our parents would be so happy too. We were both delighted and looking forward to having the baby. We continued taking our short vacations and we would send the film back to my parents for developing and for them to see what we were doing. In one of the pictures it showed Jane apparently reaching the top of a Swiss mountain with snow around her. My parents were very worried. They did not want us – mainly Jane – taking any such risks. I had to quickly explain that we were on a mountain road with large rocks on one side and I could not resist taking a picture of Jane in which she was apparently reaching the top of a mountain. No more such pictures to upset them.

During the last few months of pregnancy, Jane and I enjoyed long walks each evening, as recommended by our doctor. We would often stop in at a little pizzeria overlooking the Bay of Naples located only a 40-minute walk from our home. So we would have an inexpensive pizza with a glass of red wine and then walk back home. Our daughter Linda was born at the Naval Hospital on May 30, 1961, a very healthy, wonderful baby. It turned out that she was the 2,500th baby born at a Naval Hospital overseas. The picture appeared in Naval Times. We were both delighted and very proud parents.

6. RETURNING TO THE UNITED STATES

In an attempt to financially support the only two remaining American Flag cruise ships going trans-Atlantic – the USS Independence and the USS Constitution – the United States Congress authorized American military officers going to England or Europe on military orders to travel First Class on such voyages. As a result, there were two options for getting out of the Navy and returning to the United States. You could go back First Class by ship, which normally took nine to ten days, or you could return by military air transport. If you had a baby, to go back by ship, the baby would have to be at least six weeks old. If the baby was younger, we would have to travel by air. Luckily, Linda made that age qualification by one day, and we went back First Class on the USS Independence. It was an interesting experience going back to the United States.

The ship line told us that they had babysitters available to be with our baby so the two of us could go to dinner together. And we thought, fine! We actually did that one night and when we got back to our cabin, the babysitter was almost beside herself and said that from the moment we left to the moment we came back, the baby was constantly crying. We decided that for that trip we would not leave the baby alone again, and that we would eat separately. For breakfast or lunch it was possible to go to a buffet where we could take Linda with us, so that worked out. The three of us were together all the time for the rest of the trip, except when Jane and I took turns for dinner.

Arriving back in New York we rented a car and drove to Newport, Rhode Island to visit Jane's mother who was so delighted and proud to be a grandmother and to have such a beautiful granddaughter. I then went down to New York City when our Volkswagen came in. The few pieces of furniture that we had, the bed, the chest and the dining room table set were going to be delivered to my parents' home in Toledo, Ohio where my father was a Professor of Economics at the University of Toledo.

After picking up the car, I drove to Newport and then Jane and I drove with our daughter Linda to Toledo to spend some time with my parents. The day after we arrived, my mother asked would it be all right for her to put on the noon news. We said, "Yes, of course!" On the noon news the story of the moment was that the Administrative Assistant to the City Manager had just been fired. This was on a Tuesday. On Wednesday, I went down to City Hall and I talked with the City Manager John Alspach and I gave him my resume and I gave him Admiral Howard Yeager as my reference.

On Thursday *The Toledo Blade* called my father and asked for more details on his son Joe. On Friday morning the City Manager called and said I had the job and I was to start the following Monday. It turned out that the City Manager was a Navy Commander in WWII and was the Captain of a destroyer. Virtually, like everyone in the Navy, he had the deepest respect for Admiral Yeager. What a wonderful job it was! I am so glad that I had the job. The pay was twice as much as what I had received in the Navy. Jane said, "We will save every penny of the difference except for the income tax." And I agreed.

We looked at homes located fairly near my parent's home and we found this small home for rent. It seemed perfect for us, with two bedrooms upstairs. About 1,100 square feet, with an outside garage, likely built in the late 1920s or 1930s. I started my new job on Monday and I quickly formed a good bond with John Alspach, the City Manager. Since I had landed the job from the recommendation of Admiral Yeager, I was determined to not let Mr. Alspach down.

I would work an average of ten hours a day. Mr. Alspach treated me not only as an employee but as a friend, which was wonderful. Looking back over all the places I have worked, I am very happy to say that I have never worked for a person whom I did not highly respect and I worked hard to not let them down, including in the Navy, this job in Toledo, and future jobs with the city of Ann Arbor and in San Diego with Mercy Hospital. During our two-year stay in Toledo, our son Joseph Jr. and our son Michael were born. Now we were the proud parents of three wonderful children.

7. ANN ARBOR AND OVER A CUP OF COFFEE

After two years in Toledo, in 1963 I applied for the position of Personnel Director for the City of Ann Arbor – my home town – and I was selected for the position on the recommendation of a close friend of my parents. I knew many of the people and city employees personally as friends. The City Hall of Ann Arbor is very modern and beautiful, and Ann Arbor is a lovely town and is home to the University of Michigan. This was a job that I enjoyed immensely. In every Department of the City I had friends and it was a joy to be back there in my home town.

Jane and I were both anxious to physically move to Ann Arbor after taking the job, rather than have the 70-minute long Toledo-Ann Arbor commute each way. In looking around, I found this beautiful model home for sale in a new development on Georgetown Boulevard in the northeast part of Ann Arbor. The development was off Plymouth Road and on the other side of Plymouth Road was what would become the North Campus of the University of Michigan, which, incidentally, started with the purchase of farm land owned by my father.

The house was a beautiful two-story new home with four bedrooms, including one bedroom having its own private bathroom, all situated on a large lot. There was a brand new elementary school being built across the field from our home, which would be perfect as our family grew. There was also a community swimming pool as part of the development and that is where the kids had a fabulous time each summer. Our home and our backyard, where we established a lot of playground equipment, became a sort of center for the neighborhood children, and it was where they were always welcome to play. We did ask that they not come over until after 8am in the morning. About that time, there would be knocks on the door with kids asking if they could come over and play. It was a joy for Jane and me and for our children. So the house was perfect.

My office as Personnel Director was in the basement along with the Director of Purchasing. Also in the basement was a place for the employees to come in to have snacks and coffee. I was having coffee with a friend, and he was telling me about coming back from vacation in Traverse City, Michigan, located on Lake Michigan. He said, "The vacation was for eight days, and it rained for six days, and the cost was $400." I said, "Well there are a lot of places you can go for $400." And he commented, "Not as a black." I thought of Bermuda, where I'd gone first at age sixteen, and had also gone when returning from two of our Assault Group missions, for a few days of rest and relaxation. Bermuda was perfect because there was no racial discrimination. The Prime Minister was black, half the parliament was black. Open to everyone coming in to Bermuda – a very welcoming place.

The new hotel being built was to be called the Sonesta, a 4-Star, with water on three sides including a lovely cove with a beautiful beach. I called the manager of the hotel and asked for a rate for a group of approximately 80 coming in for a five-day visit for the month of October. He gave me the rate, and then I went to a great friend, Tom Conlin. We had grown up together, and my father and his father were very close friends. His father had died in his early 50s, as I remember. When I went to talk to him, I said, "I'd like to charter a plane for Bermuda from the Detroit airport – probably a turbo prop for 78 passengers." Tom checked and gave me the rate. I told him if we did not get the full number of passengers to pay for the charter, I would pay the difference, as I did not want him to be at risk. After this successful trip, we were moving up slowly to larger planes such as the Boeing 707 with seating capacity of 140 to 179 at that time. We used a number of airlines and one of them was Air Canada.

At the same time that I was Personnel Director of Ann Arbor, I was also in graduate school full-time and, while in graduate school, Vanderbilt was our hero. Vanderbilt started with one small shuttle boat between New York City and Stanton Island. He had the lowest rate of the shuttle boats and over time he purchased all of the other shuttle boats. Being the owner of all of the shuttle boats he did not raise the rate – kept it the same. He also earned the title of "Commodore" in New York.

Vanderbilt did the same thing with railroads – as he purchased them, he cut the profit to 5% because he knew no one could compete against him at a 5% profit. So in talking with Tom, I told him I wanted our profit to be just 5% which we would split 50/50. So our first trip was a charter to Bermuda and we would stay for five days at the Sonesta, with a rum swizzle party on arrival. Full dinner each evening with women required to wear long dresses, and men required to wear coat and tie, and a buffet breakfast every morning.

The announcement went out to the employees and the price was $195 per person. My friend – who had initially given me the idea of finding a place where everyone would be welcome and the weather would be wonderful – was one of the first to sign up along with his wife. The trip sold out in two hours, as the $195 price was less than the air rate alone to Bermuda. This was possible because it was before deregulation of airline rates. Prior to the mid-1970s all airlines had the same rate to every destination and that rate covered all of their cost. So the only cost to the airline for a charter was the cost of fuel and crew, resulting in very low rates. The trip was a complete success. Everyone loved it.

Working with Tom Conlin, a really tremendous person, we decided to have six back-to-back charters to Bermuda every fall, and the same thing to the Bahamas every spring, also for $195. We also started to have back-to-back charters to Rome and to Dublin. The rate for our back-to-back charters to Rome, staying at the 4-Star Leonardo Da Vinci Hotel, was $385 for seven nights and that included a full buffet breakfast and dinner every evening. The Leonardo Da Vinci Hotel was selected because it was perfectly located in Rome. It was half-way between the Spanish steps and the Vatican so you could walk to each. We also had back-to-back trips to Dublin, also for seven nights, staying at the Jury Hotel and that was initially $350 and Munich for seven nights was $365.

A charter would have to be with a bona fide group and was not open to just anyone. We chose groups that were open to city employees, yacht club members and Catholic Deaneries. On the weekend after the announcement had gone out, Jane and I would attend the meetings of groups that had already signed up for the tour. We would select a team of one or two couples to actually handle the program for that city group, or yacht club or Catholic Deanery and in exchange they would go for free. Jane was superb in describing the program and we both answered questions from the attendees.

Basically we had six back-to-back trips to Rome each fall, and six back-to-back trips to Dublin each spring. We also had some back-to-back trips to Munich with basically the same rate as going to Rome. Jane and I would take our children on the first trip to make sure everything went well. And so the children would go at least two times a year and often three times a year, including Munich. We also took Jane's mother to Rome and Dublin. We started this when the children were three, four and five years old. Jane dressed them immaculately, and they mingled with the local children very well. Jane deducted the full fare for her mother and our children from our 2.5% profit and Jane made sure that all of our 2.5% profit (less family deductions and the amount for income tax) would be placed in the bank and saved.

The program was so successful that Jane and I were receiving more income from the trips than from my income with the city.

Also, on the trips to Rome and to Dublin we would include four to five priests with free passage, on only one or two of the trips (not all six trips each year). This continued until we moved to La Jolla. In La Jolla we started the same thing on a much smaller scale, with a wonderful friend Don Ward of International Travel. We would do two trips to each place each year (Rome and Dublin) and it would be for members of a church in our Catholic Deanery. The rate for eight nights from San Diego to Rome was $498 and that included again staying as before at the Leonardo Da Vinci Hotel with buffet breakfast and dinner. This started in 1972. We arranged for the same rate to Dublin, also for eight nights. The more back-to-back trips we had, the less it cost us, so it was more expensive to have fewer trips. Also it was further to fly from San Diego than from the mid-west. We did not organize trips to Bermuda or the Bahamas at that time.

The rates charged on all of these charters was less than half the person would pay if they were flying to the destination on their own and staying in the same hotels. So in a sense we were able to send thousands of people to Rome and to Dublin and to Bermuda and the Bahamas for the first time who may have never gone on their own, since it would have been at two to three times the price. This was especially true for Rome. Many people would say to us that it was the best vacation they had ever had in their life. Many of the priests of the Catholic Deanery were especially appreciative, saying that they had never been to Rome.

When deregulation took place in the mid-1970s, each airline set their own rate for each destination and the competition resulted in lower rates. With deregulation it would now be more expensive to charter a plane than to fly economy class.

I will note that at the time of our move to Ann Arbor in 1963, Jane's mother was living in Newport and many of her friends were moving out of the area in which she lived. Jane's mother did not drive, so it was becoming isolating for her. We asked her if she would come and live with us, and she accepted. We gave her the bedroom with the separate bath. Jane and I both deeply loved Margaret, and it was a pure joy for us and our children to have her live with us. If the children were upset with us, they could always go and talk with her. Whether she agreed with them or not, she was always willing to listen. She lived with us until her death in 1986, almost 22 years later, when she died peacefully in our home in La Jolla.

8. MOVING TO LA JOLLA

After my first six years with the city of Ann Arbor, I was made Special Assistant to the City Manager, Guy Larcom, who had been the City Manager of Ann Arbor for almost twenty years at that point and he was a very wonderful person.

The city of Ann Arbor was changing and during the Vietnam period it became Berkeley East. There were a lot of demonstrations, with students setting buildings on fire, disruption of classes, and then two weeks before the final exams, protesting students went in as a group and vandalized the law library area, turning over all of the book racks. The city of Ann Arbor had an agreement with the University of Michigan that city police would not go on campus, since the University had their own police force. The campus police did absolutely nothing, however. Fortunately, the Ann Arbor Fire Department could go in and put out the fires set by the students.

The final blow to me was on one particular day when a Professor of Engineering, who I had known since the time I was a child – with his home only a block away from where I lived, I would go to shovel snow and mow the lawn – was attacked. This happened as he was leaving the School of Engineering in the center of the main campus where he was attacked by eight male students. While they were beating him up, a crowd of 200 gathered to cheer them on. Finally the campus police did act, but the students received no punishment. The reason he was attacked was that the Engineering Department was allowing NROTC (Naval Reserve Officer Training Corp) programs on campus, which commissioned such students as Naval Officers as soon as they graduated.

As a result of this upsetting event, I decided that we were going to move. Jane and I are very liberal, but we thought this was way over the top. We believe in public schools, so I researched and found the list of the cities with the top ten rated public schools in the United States. One was Ann Arbor, one was Palo Alto, California and one was La Jolla, California.

So Jane and I flew out to Palo Alto, which is located on inner San Francisco Bay. I interviewed with the City, and I interviewed with the County and they each made me a job offer. Asking for time for a decision, Jane and I flew to San Diego and we toured La Jolla with a realtor. Loving sailing as we did, we felt La Jolla and the nearby yacht clubs in San Diego were perfect.

Remember, in Ann Arbor we had also been involved in group charters, and thanks to Jane, all of that money from group charters had been saved. So we were in a position to look for a beautiful five-bedroom home in the village of La Jolla. Only one five-bedroom home was available and that was right across the street from the ocean, and it was too expensive for us. So we told the realtor again what we were looking for and we returned to Ann Arbor where we were going to remain for the next four months, as we wanted the children to complete the year in their elementary school. I also had to give four months notice to the City since I was the one who was negotiating with the unions.

During our few days in San Diego and La Jolla, we found the perfect street that would be ideal for us. It was an area of large lots and beautiful new homes, on a hillside of Mount Soledad and many of the homes had ocean views. A few of them were also five-bedroom homes, however none of these were for sale. This particular street was perfect because the children could walk to the elementary school, junior high and high school. I was almost ready to sign a contract to build a home in La Jolla Shores, an area where there was only an elementary school. I had the contract in my hands when I received a call from Jane at 10am which would have been 7am in California. Jane said the realtor had just called, and a house, in the exact area that we wanted, had come on the market. I called the realtor and we bought the house on that very day. This was in March 1970 so we were extremely happy. We told them we would not be moving there until the first part of July.

I flew out to San Diego and had an interview with the Human Resources Department of University of California, San Diego (in La Jolla).
I interviewed with the County and I also interviewed with Mercy Hospital and Medical Center, which is the largest hospital in the city of San Diego.

I received job offers from all three, and I accepted the offer with Mercy Hospital and Medical Center as I was so impressed with all of the wonderful things they were doing for the community. They had free clinics in Southeast San Diego, they had a large clinic as part of the hospital that was free, open to all, or partially paid depending on income. They also supported a clinic in Tijuana. I wanted to be associated with such a wonderful and caring organization. The problem was that I could not take the position until the first of July. Would they be willing to hold the position open for me? The University and County could, since they had much larger departments. To my pleasant surprise, the Hospital was willing to leave the position open for me until July, which was really wonderful.

When we moved to La Jolla in July of 1970 it was still a village. There were two feed stores with hay, alfalfa, and grain for ponies and horses, plus feed for chickens along with other farm-related items. The village's main street – Girard – was deserted after 9pm, and there were nice family-type restaurants. When we arrived in July we went to the home we had purchased in March. When we arrived at the door, the wife of the previous owner (she was co-owner) gave us a tour of the home. We felt that it was beautiful but the colors were dark – both outside and inside. When we reached the very spacious and beautiful master bedroom on the first floor, the wife said to Jane, "You are going to love this room." Jane replied, "This room is for my mother." To this the wife said, "For your mother!" – as though we were crazy. Jane and I both replied: "Yes, for our mother." Jane and I took the smallest of the four upstairs bedrooms.

La Jolla was a great place for the children to grow up. The children enjoyed the beaches and, Jane and I think, they also enjoyed sailing on Saturday when we often had neighbors and their children go with us. A professional master carpenter who had TB (tuberculosis) and was not able to do hard physical work, directed his son and me in building a very beautiful cabin on the hill in behind our home. We soon had a pony, a neighbor had a pony, and another neighbor had a donkey. Our sons Joe and Mike and I built a nice pony shed for our pony "Misty" in one day.

The village had, and still has, beautiful ocean side parks given to the village as gifts from Ellen Browning Scripps (of the Scripps-Howard newspaper chain) and by the Kellogg family. As in all of California, the beaches are all public, just as they are in Hawaii, and the many beaches were beautiful. It was a perfect place for the children to grow up. The public schools were, and are, outstanding.

The dark colors of the home, both inside and outside, were soon taken care of by Jane and me. Jane picked out the colors – all light – and the wallpaper. During our 40 years of living there, together we painted the outside of the home seven times. Jane and I worked very well as a team.

I ended up working at Mercy Hospital from 1970 to 1987. In the mid-1980s the culture of Mercy Hospital and Medical Center – the largest hospital in San Diego – began to change. Up until that time the emphasis was on providing excellent patient care while avoiding any unnecessary expenses, and extending care to those in need in the community of San Diego and across the border in Mexico. In terms of finances the feeling was truly that "God will Provide" and the financial position of the hospital was never, in my 17 years as Personnel Director, shared with the employees.

In late 1985 there was a very clear change. The hospital never had a motto, perhaps other than "Service above Self and Service to Others." Suddenly the hospital had a motto and that was "No Margin – No Mission." Again the employees received no information on the financial position of the hospital, but many of us realized that such a motto can justify all kinds of changes, as it did. As I remember, the free clinics in Southeast San Diego were quickly discontinued as were the services across the border in Tijuana, Mexico.

These changes, without explanation as to why they were done, resulted in resistance by many employees including myself. As an effective way to encourage such employees to leave, an early retirement option was offered in the spring of 1987.

The option was that employees electing early retirement would be credited with five years of additional service and the rate would be based on an additional five years of age. A number of employees, including department heads such as myself, took this option. In my case, I suddenly had 22 years of service instead of 17 and I was 56 instead of 51. The pension, with the same amount going to Jane if I died first, was – and remains – $611.45 per month.

To celebrate my early retirement, Jane and I drove up along the coast of California and Oregon. In one small Oregon town we stopped for dinner. As the waitress approached us, she said: "Do you want to see the Senior Menu?" I thought, "I guess I just retired in time."

For the first two years after leaving Mercy Hospital, Jane and I enjoyed a relaxed life, including more travel to Europe. In 1989 Jane and I started the company, Hospital Educational Services. Our goal was to produce quality educational programs for hospitals in the United States and Canada and to produce them at a cost that the smallest hospitals – such as the 40-bed hospitals – could afford. Jane was responsible for all of the business side of the company and I was responsible for creating and producing the programs. When we sold the company in 1994 we had established educational programs in over 2,500 hospitals in the United States and Canada and in over 500 Schools of Nursing.

9. GREAT EUROPEAN TRAVEL

For Jane and me, traveling together has always been an important part of our lives. We would also take delight in sharing what we had learned during our travels. As a result, Jane and I were often asked by friends to describe what we have learned about traveling to Europe and Ireland. When we were living in La Jolla, *The San Diego Union* newspaper interviewed Jane for an article about traveling to Europe. Here on the island of Kauai, Hawaii, the local newspaper – *The Garden Island* – had a two-part series on us with the title: "Europe: Twice the Fun – Half the Price." Well, these are the things we have learned.

To Go With Friends

We have learned to go with friends, both to share the costs and to share the adventure. Both Jane and I are "people persons" and enjoy being with others. Going with friends is also the least expensive way to travel in Europe. We would usually travel with two other couples and rent a six-passenger van. Now, the least expensive vans (which we always took) are quite a bit smaller than our vans here in the United States. As a result, the luggage space – in back of the third row of seats – is small and there is only space for six carry-on bags. Except for our many earlier days of charter flights (in the 1960s to the mid-1970s) where we were responsible for the flights, Jane and I always traveled with just a carry-on bag each – plus a small camera bag for me and a large purse for Jane. Truly, it is not a problem, even on a 15-night cruise to Europe. Plus, the benefit is you always have your luggage with you.

To Research Low Cost Airfares

We have often used www.priceline.com to bid for our flights to Munich, London (Gatwick Airport), Paris, Brussels, and Rome. We bid at 60% (including taxes and airport fees) of the current lowest rate and we have always been successful with the these airports but we have never been successful with flights to Ireland. We should point out that we travel in late March, April, May and early June, or late September and October, thus avoiding the expense of the peak season travel. We fly mid-week and we also, if possible, check for the "real" load factor (current passengers booked) rather than believe in the "just two seats left." From California it is about six to seven thousand miles to Europe and there are many direct flights from the Los Angeles airport and from the San Francisco airport. From Hawaii you first fly to a destination on the "mainland" and fly to Europe from there.

Jane and I love staying in Bed & Breakfast homes in villages and in a farm house. In virtually all Bed & Breakfast homes the family is very welcoming and the other guests are friendly and are happy to share their experiences with you.

We rarely book a Bed & Breakfast room in advance but rather we start looking for a Bed & Breakfast around 3pm in the afternoon and are successful 95% of the time. In France, Bed & Breakfast homes will have a sign CHAMBERS in the window. In Germany the sign will be ZIMMER and in England and Ireland the sign will be B&B or BED AND BREAKFAST. You can also use the internet and request a list of various Bed & Breakfast homes by naming the village, town or city. In addition, many tourist area villages have a Tourist Information booth and they will have a full listing of area Bed & Breakfast homes and they are happy to call the home to check on room availability. Since we only traveled during off-season or mid-season periods, it was never a problem to find lodging.

There are also times when we stay at very attractive (but much less expensive for the area) hotels. Our three favorite "budget buster" hotels are: Hotel Miralago, located in the lovely village of Cernobbio on beautiful Lake Como in northern Italy. Lake Como is one of the most beautiful places on earth and the Hotel Miralago is a gem. Great staff and superb buffet breakfast. The daily rate is almost $200 but that is half of what you would pay for a similar (but we think not as nice) hotel in the nearby town of Como.

Our second "budget buster" hotel is Hotel Silla in Florence, Italy. This hotel is fantastic. It is in a lovely villa on the quiet side of the river and it is only a 15-minute walk to the center of Florence. It is family-owned, the rooms are lovely and the breakfast is superb. The daily rate is approaching the $200 figure but the hotel is nicer than the hotels in the very center of Florence where most similar hotels charge $350 to $400 per night and in the center of Florence it is very easy to feel crowded.

Our third "budget buster" hotel is the Hotel Alimanda in Rome. It is a family-owned hotel and the family is great. It is just a 3-minute walk to the entrance of the Sistine Chapel. Weather permitting, there is a wonderful buffet breakfast on the roof patio where you are overlooking the Vatican wall. Again, as before, the per night cost approaches $200. The first time Jane and I were there we had our car parked in a nearby garage they owned or had rented. When we were checking out I pointed out that the bill did not include the cost of the garage parking. The owner's brother put his hand on my shoulder and said, "Joe, this time it's free. Next time we charge double."

In addition to these three "budget busters" there are three great hotel choices that Jane and I love and they are not expensive.

The first is Hotel Cristallo in Lido Venice which was recommended to us by a good friend. Lido Venice is a small town on an island just east (seaward) of Venice. The island has lovely beaches and a tiny airfield (for small private planes only). While Venice seems to be about 80% tourists, Lido Venice seems about 80% residents and 20% tourists – a very nice change. While we once stayed in Venice, we found the prices very high and the crowds of people to be almost overwhelming. Lido Venice has constant ferry service to Venice and it makes many stops there. These ferries are like buses and are inexpensive if you buy a pass for three or five days. You can take a ferry and tour all of the areas of Venice and then come back to peaceful Lido Venice where hotel and outdoor restaurant prices are very reasonable. The Hotel Cristallo is located on the town's main street – where there are many outdoor restaurants – and is just a 5-minute walk to the ferry landing. The spring and fall prices are about $130 per night and include a nice breakfast.

The second great and reasonably-priced hotel is the Hotel Reine D'azur in the French Riviera village of Roquebrune-Cap-Martin. The village adjoins the town of Merton and the hotel and overlooks the sea. It is a 10-minute drive around the Cap to Monaco and yet it is a different world of peace and a much more relaxing pace. The village and Merton are gems. They are right on the water and Merton has beautiful waterfront parks, free street parking (except by the parks) and a working boat type small harbor with an ancient fortress overlooking the harbor. The coastal drive to Monaco, Villefranche, Nice, and Cannes is breathtaking, as are the very winding drives on the hills above. The mid-season daily rate for a room with a balcony overlooking the beach and including breakfast is about $140. There are also nearby inexpensive restaurants located just above the beach.

Our third best buy is in one of the world's most famous resorts – that is, St. Moritz. Jane and I strongly recommend the 2-Star Hotel Bellaval. In St. Moritz there is a narrow two-lane road going around part of the beautiful lake. The Hotel Bellaval is right on that road at the entrance to the lake. It is the closest hotel on the lake with the finest views of the lake over all the other hotels in St. Moritz. There are rooms with a private bathroom and there are others using shared bathrooms. I believe that the hotel has about 25 rooms of which five are double rooms with balconies and private bath rooms. Ask for Room 23. It is almost two rooms with a 14-foot long,

4-foot wide balcony where you feel you are almost over the lake.

Our favorite picture of that European trip is of Jane at a table on the balcony with a peanut butter sandwich in one hand, a glass of wine in the other and the beautiful lake in the background. The cost for this room per night with breakfast is about $135. The St. Moritz rail station is directly in back of this hotel but trains are all electric and you hear nothing.

FOR EUROPEAN HOTELS IT IS BEST TO BOOK DIRECTLY WITH THE HOTEL AS MOST INTERNET TRAVEL SITES ADD ANOTHER 10% OR MORE TO THE BILL.

European River/Canal Cruises

Here you have the option of taking a canal or river cruise. Jane and I took a wonderful river cruise a number of years ago on the Danube with eight other friends from our All Hallows Catholic Parish in La Jolla, California. We went on the Peter Dahlman line which was a German line, and we all had a wonderful time. The beautiful river vessel was underway during the day and we were able to enjoy the beautiful views we were passing and then we would stop at a village or small town for the night and enjoy touring in that village or town the next day. The food was great and the breakfast buffet also had champagne. What a nice way to start the day. I think that our per person rate (in today's dollars) was about $110. Sadly, that company has gone out of business. The current per person rate on such a river cruise line is between $250 to $350 per person per day. Very expensive.

So, there is an alternative. That is to take a self-operated river cruise vessel on the canals of Europe. Hopefully, among your friends there is one who has some experience with power boats and hopefully all of you have the spirit of adventure that it takes. Jane certainly had that spirit of adventure and we decided to take a self-operated cruise boat out of the lovely town of Sneek in Friesland, now a province of the Netherlands. Two couples said that they would like to go. One couple was great at sailing but knew nothing about power boats. The other couple had been on a friend's power boat "a number of times" so we were set.

On a spring day we flew into Brussels, rented a small van and headed up to Sneek – a beautiful small town. Ahead of time, I knew the boat we would be renting and I had polo shirts with the name *MV Mistral* made up in advance. I took the boat out under observation to check out the boat and passed with flying colors. We were off and for a week and – except the time we were almost killed, as you will read about in the chapter "My Guardian Angel" – we had a wonderful adventure. Friesland is different for renting a self-operated canal boat as there are no locks to encounter. There are bridges, where we needed to wait for someone to raise them, but that is a small problem. We had a fabulous time and we tied up at beautiful parks at various villages and towns and we almost felt like "locals" going to the restaurants and mingling with the people.

As we finished the cruise we felt pride in being able to do it ourselves. In converting the value of the dollar then to today – compared to the Euro – our person per day cost was $63 and, even adding $30 for food and dinner ashore, the cost was still less than $100 per person per day.

Least Expensive Cruises

Trans-Atlantic cruise ship fares are often the best bargain one can ever get on a European vacation as some trans-Atlantic cruises have a large number of stops at various European ports. For us, the mid-size ships (carrying 2,200 passengers or less) are best.

Attitude

Finally, the last thing to share about what we learned is the importance of attitude. An ancient Greek philosopher said: "Some people can make a heaven out of hell. Others can make a hell out of heaven." It is something Jane and I would think about as we invited others to join us. It is important that those with us accept and enjoy the often modest places where we stay during our trips to Europe. Keeping that in mind in selecting trip-mates, we always had a wonderful time together and enjoyed all of the places and all of our varied experiences.

10. TWENTY-ONE DAYS OF TRAVEL

In 1977 Delta Airlines made an astonishing offer. The offer was "Fly Delta for Twenty-One Days to any destination for $199." The only limitation was that you could not fly to any one destination more than once. What a wonderful offer. When Jane and I looked at that offer, we both said, "Let's Go!"

At Mercy Hospital and Medical Center I had an outstanding Assistant Director of Personnel and I was able to take time off without pay. We told our three children about the offer and we described what we wanted to do. We also asked a niece, Cindy Frisinger, if she would come with us. She would be a wonderful person to room with Linda.

We wanted to take the first Delta flight out on the morning of the first day – regardless of its destination – and the very last flight back to San Diego on the twenty-first day, regardless of where it was coming from. Our trip was from Thursday, July 27 to Thursday, August 17, 1978.

So, this is what we did.

On Day One, the first Delta flight that day was going to New Orleans. Landing in New Orleans we took a Delta flight on to San Juan, Puerto Rico. We stayed there for three days at the Hilton, right on the beach in San Juan. On the morning of Day Four – a Sunday – we took the short flight to St. Thomas. In St. Thomas we took a cab to church for Mass. At Mass we asked the usher if there was a grocery store open as we had chartered a 42-foot sailboat for three days and we wanted to buy food for that trip. The usher happened to be the Director of Tourism for the island. He told us that only one grocery store was open on Sunday and he said that our cab driver – who was waiting for us – would know the way there.

After Mass we went to the grocery store and purchased food and then went to the harbor and checked out the 42-foot boat we had chartered. Jane and I were experienced sailors as we had sailed various sizes of boats ever since we were married, so we passed the "check out" sail. By noon we were underway and we sailed to the island of St. John, in the US Virgin Islands. During the sail we had to keep a look-out on the bow as there are coral towers to avoid. Once in Caneel Bay, out from the 5-Star Caneel Bay Resort, we prepared to anchor. The water was crystal clear. We put out 50 feet of anchor cable and line and it did not reach the sea floor. We went in closer and tried it again with the same result. Finally on the third try the cable and line reached the sea floor at 30 feet so we put out 100 feet of line and anchored safely. Just to see how crystal clear the water was, we dropped a dollar bill over the side and as it slowly went down and reached the sea floor, we could read the dollar bill clearly. Our son Mike leaned over to look and his glasses fell off. The water was so clear that the glasses looked within reach – but none of us could have dove down that deep. On the shore was the famous 5-Star Caneel Bay Resort. Our charter sailboat had an Avon small boat that we could take to the beach so we did that and had lunch at the Caneel Bay Resort. We enjoyed the beach and the peacefulness of the bay. We stayed at anchor there for two nights and returned to St. Thomas where we stayed on board for the third night.

On the seventh day, we flew from Saint Thomas to Miami and then to Detroit to attend a Frisinger Family Reunion. Landing in Detroit we rented a car and reached the nice motel where we would stay for three nights. The Family Reunion was at my Frisinger grandparents' cabin on North Lake, a lake near Ann Arbor, and it was a wonderful all-day event.

On the tenth day we took a Delta flight from Detroit to Burlington, Vermont. Jane said, "We've never been to northern Vermont, let's stop there." We stayed there one night.

On the eleventh day we flew to Bermuda with a stop in Boston. (A stop at an airport going on to another airport does not count in the limitation rule.) In Bermuda we stayed at the Sonesta Hotel (the same hotel that we used for charters in the 1960s). We stayed at this beautiful hotel for four nights. It is elegant and women (girls too) have to wear long dresses for dinner and men (boys too) have to wear coat and tie.

On the fifteenth day we flew to Boston where Jane's niece Janet and her husband Brian gave us an "official" welcome as Brian was on the staff of the Mayor of Boston. Brian was a graduate of Harvard and was also the Captain of the football team. In addition to being on the Mayor's staff, he was also getting his Master's Degree in Business. From Boston we rented a car and drove to Newport where we stayed for the next three days. Newport is Jane's home town and also our children, Linda, Joe and Mike had been there many times before. For Cindy it was her first trip to Newport so we had the joy of showing her the many sights of beautiful Newport.

On the eighteenth day we flew from Boston to Denver where we rented a car and drove to Fort Collins, Colorado where my mother was living and where my brother and his wife and their four children (including Cindy) also lived. It was nice to be with family. We stayed there for three nights.

Remember, we wanted to take the first Delta flight out of San Diego and to take the last Delta flight landing in San Diego on the final day. The last flight going to San Diego on the twenty-first day was a flight from Atlanta. So, on that twenty-first day Cindy stayed in Fort Collins and we flew first from Denver to Atlanta and then took the flight from Atlanta to San Diego.

Just like that!

11. JANE'S LIFE AND SPIRIT OF ADVENTURE

Jane Elizabeth Scanlon was born at home in Taunton, Massachusetts on March 13, 1932, the daughter of Margaret Ann Feeney Scanlon and Edward Scanlon. Jane had an older brother, Robert Francis Scanlon who was born on February 14, 1927.

When she was a young girl, the family moved to Newport, Rhode Island where her father Edward was a molder in the Naval Torpedo Factory located on an island in Newport Harbor. The factory had been built on an island in the event that if there was an explosion, no civilians or non-employees would be killed. It was rather dangerous work.

In Newport Jane attended elementary school, middle school and Rogers High School. The entire family loved living in Newport. They lived in housing that was built by the Navy for employees of the Navy, the Torpedo Factory and other Naval facilities. Bob, who was five years older than Jane, was a lifeguard at Easton's Beach in Newport during the summer, and he was second in command of the Military Cadet Program at Rogers High School. Jane graduated from Rogers High School where she had been one of the leaders in the Hospitality Committee and also active in various plays. Both Bob and Jane were on the Honor Roll and maintained almost all A marks at Rogers High School.

As a molder, Jane's father was generally working with lead. As a result, he developed lung cancer and was ill for a number of years. Jane would visit him every day when he was in the Newport Hospital. He died at the age of 51.

While Jane had outstanding grades, she said that one of the hardest days in her life was when she went to tell her High School Guidance Counselor that she was not going on to college, but instead was working for the New England Telephone Company for New England Bell there in Newport. She was not able to go on to college because her brother had been in the Army Air Force toward the end of World War Two and since he was then attending a university on Long Island, New York, Jane became the breadwinner for her mother and herself. Jane accepted that assignment without any complaint. Working at the telephone company on the switchboard, Jane did an outstanding job and her managers recommended her for a promotion working in the office. Jane took the promotion, but found she was not one who enjoyed telling people that their telephone was going to be disconnected, so she asked to go back to the switchboard.

Jane was a very caring person and very thoughtful of others. She attended mass every Sunday and was also active in her Catholic church. Jane loved being in Newport and she felt so lucky to be there. She developed a number of friendships and she said that in Newport you can go anywhere on a bicycle, which was very true. Being the source of income for herself and her mother, Jane took many extra days of work and she saved all of the money from those extra days. Employees of New England Telephone Company also had the opportunity to buy stock at a reduced price. Jane would always buy stock when it was available. If some of her friends did not want to buy, she would buy their shares. Jane was a great money-saver.

In Newport, if you are a local, you are really taken care of – whether at a store, a restaurant, or at an event – you would get preference.

For example, Jane and other local girls were outside of St. Mary's Church when the Kennedy wedding was taking place. The police officer at the door of the church recognized that the girls there were all Newport girls and he said they could come in and stand in the back. So they were able to attend the Kennedy wedding. Being local meant a lot to the residents of Newport.

On our very first drive, on the day after I met her, Jane and I were taking the beautiful Ocean Drive, which is approximately ten miles in length, with many curves and also views of the mansions and a wonderful State Park. Jane knew all the history of Newport. On our first drive, we stopped and Jane pointed out two small rocks in the bay just off shore. The rocks were about six to seven feet apart. Jane said that for an Indian to prove his love for a maiden he would prove it by jumping from one rock to the other. I then said, "I'll do that for you." And Jane quickly replied, "No, no!" I probably would have killed myself trying, but I was very willing to try.

The Newport Ocean Drive has a very special place in our hearts. During the remaining three and a half weeks of this time that I had left to complete the Naval Justice Training School, we would take that drive together each of those days. Over the years when we would return to Newport on vacation, we would always take the same drive every day then too. It was "Our Drive."

One of the wonderful traits that Jane had was the spirit of adventure. Whether it was in our travel, or in sailing, or in planning for exotic trips. Interestingly enough, Jane had never stepped aboard a sailboat in Newport, considered – at least by Newporters – as the sailing capital of the United States. This was quickly corrected. On our third day of marriage we were in Bermuda and that morning we took a harbor tour on a sailboat. Jane fell in love with sailing and thought it was wonderful. That is why we bought the tiny sailboat (for $175) in Naples.

When we returned to the United States, and over the years, we had a variety of sailboats. The first sailboat we purchased in Ann Arbor was a 1936, 13-foot Old Town Lapstrake Sailboat. A wooden Lapstrake Sailboat is very unique because when it is out of the water for a number of months, as it would be in Michigan, it dries out. When it's put back in the water, it leaks like a sieve for about the first two weeks. After that, it swells up enough that it will stay dry and is sailable again. In our marriage we have gone through a number of sailboats. After three years with the Old Town, we sold it and purchased a fiberglass 14-foot Rhodes Bantam.

Our next sailboat was very different. Chris Craft was a producer of very high end power boats. Back in the late 1960s they also decided to build very elegant sailboats designed by the prestigious firm of Sparkman and Stephens. As a result, they encouraged their dealers and the dealers of other power boat companies to take one of each of the three models they were making. One was a 27-foot sailboat, one was a 32-foot sailboat and one was a 36-foot sailboat.

A dealer in Detroit who carried Bertram Power Boats and Grand Banks' trawler boats did purchase one each of these beautifully designed sailboats. Jane and I went to this power boat dealer's huge warehouse where, among all of the power boats, they had the 32-foot sailboat and the 36-foot sailboat designed by Sparkman and Stephens. We thought the 32-foot boat was absolutely beautiful. It had sleeping for five persons and the entire boat looked perfect. The price was $17,500. We told the dealer how impressed we were with the boat, but the absolute top price we could pay was $12,800 which would buy a 27-foot sailboat that we had been considering. The dealer asked, "How much did you say?" And I replied, "$12,800." "Sold!" said the dealer, "I never want to have another sailboat in this warehouse, ever!" So we had this magnificent sailboat at this great discount. This was in the winter of 1969-70.

In moving to La Jolla, we had the sailboat trucked out and taken to a boat yard on Shelter Island in San Diego, and it was outfitted and put in the water there. Upon our arrival in La Jolla, we joined Silver Gate Yacht Club, located on Shelter Island, which was considered the "working man's yacht club" in San Diego.

We had this beautiful boat for a total of seven years and, except when we were on vacation, we would sail with our children every Saturday and we would often invite neighbors and their children to join us. Sometimes we would sail to nearby Glorietta Bay and anchor for the night and then return to our slip early Sunday morning in time for us all to go to Mass.

Seven years later the children reached the age when they wanted to do other things on Saturday. Jane and I understood that perfectly. We had our boat hauled out each year for the bottom to be painted. On that seventh year a yacht salesman said he had a customer who would love to buy the boat. We sold the boat to him for $15,800. We were then looking for a smaller boat, around 23 or 24 feet. By that time, Jane was a better and more aggressive sailor than I was. She would often say, "Pull in that line, I think we can go faster!" As we looked at boats, Jane was the one at the tiller doing the testing. On some of the boats, she would turn the tiller and nothing would happen for a few minutes, being so sluggish and slow.

We then heard about a 23-foot Ranger that was apparently spectacular. The boat was designed by Gary Mull who was considered one of the top sailboat designers in the country. He was located in San Francisco and in *The San Francisco Chronicle* he had a monthly column, "Mulling over Coffee." In one of those interviews he was asked, "Of all the sailboats you've designed, which one is your favorite?" This question was put to a person who had designed a number of fine, fast, large racing sailboats and a few smaller boats. Without hesitation, Gary Mull replied, "The Ranger 23."

So we drove up to the nearest Ranger dealer located at Balboa Island, near Newport Beach, California. When we took the Ranger 23 out for a test sail, Jane said, "This is perfect." The Ranger 23 had both high performance and high safety. One had been sailed around the world. Jane selected it and it proved to be a boat we both loved. With Jane's skill we could sail it right into our slip – dropping sails at exactly the right time – and make the 180-degree turn in the boat's own length, docking perfectly. Anyone unfamiliar with Jane's ability to bring the boat in safely was wondering if the boat would crash. She always brought it in perfectly.

We named each of our sailboats *GIANNA*, from the first 12-foot sailboat to the last (Ranger 23), which is "Jane" in Italian. On the 23-foot sailboat, before sailing it down to San Diego, we had the name *GIANNA San Diego* (the home port), placed on the stern in gold letters. When we went to take the boat, one of the yard crew said, "You know, when John Wayne walked by, he looked at the boat and said, 'That is beautiful.'" Good endorsement! We had that boat for 25 years and except for one trip up to Santa Catalina Island, we just sailed locally, every Saturday.

We loved sailing on our own, though we would still invite guests, usually only two people, since the boat was smaller.

We would often go out to sea, and sometimes, when coming in, the wind would drop and I would paddle the boat in with a long paddle and this could take us two to three hours. Great exercise. We had an outboard motor, but we kept it safely at home in the garage. Sailboats and power boats would pass us, and ask us if we needed a tow, however we always respectfully declined and took it in ourselves.

Another example of Jane's spirit of adventure was when we traveled with Jane's mother and the children to Maui in the Hawaiian Islands. At the time, Maui was not highly developed and there was a two-lane road that went all around the island. We decided we wanted to take that road because we wanted to see the waterfalls on the north shore and we wanted to visit Charles Lindbergh's Grave.

About a quarter of the way into the drive, there was a sign: *Wash out, road closed.* Jane looked ahead and saw that there were a lot of rocks on both sides of the road. She said to the boys and me, "Let's get out and fill all of those holes with rocks and then we can drive through." In twenty minutes we had all of the holes filled, and while it was a little rough, we drove on and we were able to go all around the island. The highlight was visiting Lindbergh's grave. We found the country lane, and walked to the beautiful church overlooking the ocean. It was a very small church, with no electricity, and candles at night.

Lindbergh was the first man to fly across the Atlantic. When Lindbergh was nearing death, he was at his home in Long Island. Juan Trippe, the President of Pan American Airlines, was a good friend of Lindbergh's and he knew that Lindbergh wanted to be buried at this church near their home at Hana in Maui. So Juan Trippe ordered one of his planes to take Lindbergh and his family, with his compliments, back to Maui. And that's where Lindbergh peacefully died. Our understanding was that he had been buried in a wooden coffin with six of the neighborhood residents having served as pall bearers. There's a tombstone with the years of his birth and death, with the inscription *...If I take the wings of the morning, and dwell in the uttermost parts of the sea...* Thanks to Jane's spirit of adventure, we were probably in the only car that drove around the island that day.

Jane and I have been blessed with three wonderful children. Our daughter, Linda, was born on May 30, 1961, our son, Joseph Jr., was born on May 27, 1962, and our son, Michael, was born on June 26, 1963. Clearly they were close and they had the advantage that they always had someone to play with "about their own age." Jane's mother, Margaret, came to live with us in 1964 and it was wonderful to have her there with us.

The children were initially growing up in a new subdivision in Ann Arbor where some of our neighbors were also families with young children. Plus there was a community swimming pool to enjoy during the summer. Our children started going with us on the charters to Europe when they were just four, five and six. On these trips they would enjoy playing with the local children – especially in Italy and they were quick to pick up some of the language. Linda was especially fast in picking up Italian and she would write, among other things – in one of her school assignments about "what you can do" – "I can speak Italian" and she could. Perhaps it was the fact that she was born there, so she is an Italian as well as being an American.

On these trips to Europe our fellow passengers were so very impressed with how well our children behaved and how neatly they were dressed, for which Jane gets complete credit. In the years 1965 to 1970 the children had been to Europe (including Ireland) five times and they had been to the Bahamas four times. Our trips to Europe with the children continued three more times in the 1970s – with the last time being for five weeks. On a number of our trips to Europe, Jane's mother would go with us, which was very nice.

On our five-week trip to Europe, Jane and I felt that it would probably be the last time the children would want to go with us – and would prefer to spend time with their friends. As a result, we were determined to show them as much of Europe during those five weeks as we could. We visited the beaches where our troops had landed on the beaches of Normandy toward the end of World War Two and we were amazed by what a challenge that was for our troops facing incoming fire from the built-in German bunkers. We also visited Paris for two days – during one of which we received a parking ticket. Paris had just gone from parking meters to a central booth where you would pay for parking, receive a slip of paper noting the number of hours credit and you were to place that slip on the window of your car. I did mail in the ticket with a check in United States dollars equal to the French currency. When we returned to the United States we had a letter from the Chief of Police of Paris. He wrote that he realized that we were tourists and the parking system was new. As a result he wrote that "I take great pleasure in returning your check and I thank you for visiting Paris." What a wonderful, thoughtful thing to do. Viva the French.

At the end of that five-week trip the children felt the trip was great but it was two weeks too long. They were probably right.

In La Jolla the children all enjoyed the beach and the public high school was rated as one of the top ten high schools in the nation. On the street where we lived the children could walk to the elementary school, middle school, and high school. The mothers as a group, however, thought the walk up a steep hill to the elementary school was perhaps too much for the kids so they formed a car pool to take them up.

After high school, Linda chose to go to the University of Santa Clara – a highly-rated Jesuit school. Our son Joe decided to go to San Diego State University. Our son Mike went to a local community college. Both Linda and Joe graduated from their schools and Linda went on to get a Master's Degree. Mike decided to look for and find exotic cars in some farmer's barn and then detail them and sell them – often for a large profit.

Our children are now scattered around the country. Our son Joe is married and with his wife Shannon they have three sons. Our daughter, Linda, is single and she lives in a beautiful townhouse in Raleigh, North Carolina. Our son Mike is also single and he lives in Scottsdale, Arizona.

Jane and I have always been very proud of our children and you will see many pictures of them in this book. I also want to tell you, the reader, that Jane made a wonderful hundred-page booklet for each of the children which included an overview of their life from the time they were born to about the late 1980s when she prepared it. The book started with their birth certificate, their papers, tests and the drawings they made in elementary school, pictures of them on our trips, the history of their grandparents and their parents. Pictures of where they lived, their dog and their pony. The book informs them of their lives and the lives of those before them.

Jane and I never wanted to be apart. However, when our daughter, Linda, decided to move from La Jolla to Raleigh, North Carolina in 2004, we both were concerned about a girl driving alone across country. I asked Jane about what she would think of me asking Linda if I could go with her and then fly back home. Jane said, "I think that's wonderful. I was worried about her driving alone, too." I told Jane that I would call her each night and Jane said that she would keep a note each day as she waited for my call. As Linda and I were driving east I felt sadness with each mile, and I was so glad to talk with Jane each evening. Her note was "… but I feel lost and tears come to my eyes many times through the day. I look forward to your call tonight. I miss you so much."

12. JOE'S LIFE

This is a review of My Life and Career, and how meeting Jane changed my life so wonderfully. After meeting Jane it was Our Lives, which is being thoroughly covered in this book.

I was born on May 25, 1934 in Frankfort, Michigan in a home overlooking Lake Michigan. I was a very fortunate child. I had wonderful loving parents (Hubert and Gwen), a wonderful brother (Howard) and wonderful grandparents (Werner and Mabel Hinterman on my mother's side and R.N. and Destina Frisinger on my father's side). My mother's father was a Methodist Minister in northern Michigan and he moved to Ann Arbor so his children could attend the University of Michigan, and he became a bus driver.

My grandfather Frisinger had a highway construction company, building highways throughout the Midwest, and primarily in Michigan, as during the depression Michigan was still thriving, thanks to the auto industry, especially Ford Motor Company. With cars, you needed highways. My Frisinger grandparents had six boys. My father Hubert was the eldest, and the three oldest boys were assigned to supervise highway construction projects in various places in Michigan, Ohio and in Illinois. My father was the one supervising the highway project near the town of Frankfort.

I am very proud of my grandparents and I was very close to both of my grandfathers. My grandfather Frisinger would take me with him out to his farm – about 18 miles out of town – three times each week during the summer from the time I was eleven to the time I was fifteen. It was on the farm that I learned to drive a tractor and I also learned the importance of caring for the land. During the seven years – from 1963 to 2000 – that I was employed by the City of Ann Arbor, I would meet my grandfather Hinterman for lunch every Thursday at the Methodist Church hall where their Men's Club had their weekly luncheon. When a black was proposed for membership my grandfather made an outstanding support speech and the man was welcomed as a member. I also learned a great lesson from my grandparents and that is that having money is not necessary to have happiness. One can have much and be happy and one can have much less and be equally happy.

When I was born I was the second son of my parents, with my brother Howard being born on Feb 28, 1933. It's my understanding that during my early months of life I was crying a great deal. At one point my parents put me in the local hospital because they thought I had croup. When they came in to see me, they saw me crying on a hard pad and my arms and my legs were tied down on the pad. They immediately took me home.

Our home town was Ann Arbor, Michigan, and my parents Hubert and Gwen Frisinger were both graduates of the University of Michigan and we were living in an apartment near the campus. When I was age three we moved to a lovely home in a nice part of Ann Arbor and that remained our home throughout our childhood, including the time at the University.

I can remember back to age three. At that age, I started to stutter and it became quite severe. This continued until age eight when I was completely cured, thanks to weekly sessions with members of the University of Michigan Speech Therapy Department – considered at that time as the best in the nation. Between ages three and five only my mother and my brother could understand me when I spoke. Even to this day, though, I am unable to say either word – stutter or stutterer – I can only spell it aloud. I don't know why.

Growing up, I always felt that I was not good enough. I would say to myself, many times each day, "I've got to be better." My parents were wonderful, and my brother is a person who I have admired all of my life. He was a leader in many things and he was always getting great grades. I was and I remain very proud of him. My grades were not good, and apparently my behavior when I was very young was not very good either. Among my 26 cousins, I was the only one who had a choice: "Do you want the spanking before we go out or when we come home?" And sometimes I would take it before I went out and then I would be very quiet when we were out. My parents were very fair and I'm sure I deserved all of those spankings, but it did fortify my belief that I was not good enough. Later I even felt that way in the Navy. My dream was that the easiest way to be nominated for a Congressional Medal of Honor is to throw yourself on the grenade and save the team, which had to be during war time. So on each of my missions going out, I could envision war occurring and I could envision a grenade coming in to our boat and I could see myself throwing myself on it. I could also envision my parents, my grandparents, my brother in his Air Force uniform and his wife, Mim, in the President's oval office, and I could hear the President say to my mother as he walked toward her, "On behalf of a grateful nation ..." And I would die very happy. And they would say, "He turned out okay."

My feeling of never being good enough continued until Jane and I married, at which time the feeling went away. During the time I was married to Jane, I never felt that I was not good enough. Since Jane's death, that feeling is with me again, though, every moment of every day.

In kindergarten none of the other children teased me and if I felt very sad my wonderful kindergarten teacher Miss Shadowiat would put me on her lap and I would feel better. By the time I reached the third grade, my speech was much better and I could speak normally. However, I had one major problem. Unless I was in the first or second row in the classroom, I could not read what the teacher was writing on the board. So I would look at my classmate's paper to see what was on the board, or ask them and my teacher would frequently say, "Frisinger, to the Principal's office." I have never cheated on anything in my life, and that's not what I was doing when looking at a classmate's paper, I simply couldn't see the board. I spent a lot of time in the Principal's office. Later, one of my uncles, who had been in the army during World War Two said to me, "Joe, we had more letters from you than from anyone else and I thank you for the letters, but they all began the same way, 'I'm in the Principal's office again...'" This problem continued until the second semester of eighth grade. There were some advantages with extremely poor eyesight in terms of popularity, in that I could not recognize people's faces unless they were very close to me. So I assumed everyone was a friend, and I would say "Good morning" or "Hi" to every student in elementary school and junior school up to the middle of eighth grade.

In the eighth grade English class, I would frequently go up from my seat to the blackboard and kneel down to write on my paper whatever was written on the board. That English teacher would kid me, and to the class she would often say, "Here comes our praying student, again." I was so embarrassed by this, that I never went up to the board again. I just stopped learning what she was teaching. I still do not know what a verb or an adverb is, or the difference between "than" or "then" and I just gave up on that class. As a result, I received a D- for English that year.

One day in that year, my father and I went to the University of Michigan League, a cafeteria on campus open to the public, to have lunch and we were waiting for my grandfather to arrive. We were sitting about 30 feet away from the door when a person came in and I asked my father, "Is that grampa?" It turned out the person was a woman, wearing a dark dress. Right after lunch, my father took me to the ophthalmologist to have my eyes tested. The ophthalmologist tested my eyes and found that my vision was 20/200. They fitted me with a pair of glasses, and as I looked out the window of the ophthalmologist's room, my first remark was, "Trees have leaves!" I knew there were leaves, but when I had looked at a tree I just saw a green ball. This perhaps partially explains why my grades were generally never above a C in elementary school or in junior high. My grades improved in high school, but when I graduated in 1952 my grades were clearly not high enough to go into the University of Michigan.

For my first two years of college I went to Ohio Wesleyan College, a small Methodist-based college in Delaware, Ohio. It was an excellent beginning, because all of the classes were conducted by professors. The classes were small and the professors were outstanding. At the University of Michigan at that time, often in a freshman and sophomore year, the instructor would be a student working on a PhD, and also the classes would often be much larger.

After my sophomore year I was able to get into the University of Michigan and I graduated from the University of Michigan in June 1956. During those final two years I was taking 20 hours each semester (normal average was 15 hours) and I had three part-time jobs. One was a volunteer job with the Michigan Daily, the University of Michigan newspaper. The second job was doing the midnight news, Monday through Friday, for the local radio station and I would be able to do it from the Michigan Daily news office, next to a teletype machine that continuously had the latest news. There would be whistles: one whistle would be a minor news story, and four whistles would be a major disaster. I would then ride my bike home by 12:40am and I would get up at 6:30am because I almost always had an 8am class. My third job was serving as a janitor on Saturday at my grandfather's office complex. It was my job to clean the floor, pick up all the papers, empty the trash cans, straighten up the desks, wash the windows and get the office ready for the coming week. It was a six to eight-hour job.

After graduating from the University of Michigan, I entered the Officer Training Program for the Navy and received my commission as an Ensign. The normal assignment is aboard ship, however there are three areas of volunteer service in which danger is high. The three areas are Aviation, Submarine and the Assault Group. The Naval Assault Group consisted of three sections. The first was Beach Jumpers, the second was Boat Unit, and the third was Underwater Demolition Team (UDT). Thinking that the Beach Jumpers sounded like the most dangerous and most interesting unit, I volunteered for that. I did not get that assignment. I asked why, and I was told, "Because you are not an electrical engineer." I did not learn until 25 years later what the Beach Jumpers really did, because we never saw them. They seemed to be in a secret area. No one would tell me what they did. As it turned out, you had to be an electrical engineer to be in the Beach Jumpers, because you never jumped on a beach. Instead, you were on a decoy vessel that had all of the electronic equipment for the radar and sonar image of every Navy ship, and used it to confuse the enemy.

So then I selected the Boat Unit, which had been created after the landing at Normandy. When Navy vessels were ready to launch a major attack, they would put the army fighters in up to 60 M8 amphibious boats. These boats would each carry up to 48 soldiers from the larger ships and they would go to the beach, lower the ramp and the soldiers would disembark. During Normandy all of the boats were under heavy fire coming in. A number of the boat crews would lower the ramp before hitting the beach. The soldiers would go out and they would all drown. Hundreds of soldiers drowned in this way. While this information was not released to the public, the Navy vowed this would never happen again. When the boats go in for a landing, all of the boats are going to hit the beach before lowering their ramps.

So the Navy created this elite force called the Boat Unit in the Assault Group that would lead these boats going in for major landings. The lead boat would be manned by an Assault Group officer and crew and have a flag to mark it. Each one of these lead boats would lead in 12 to 20 boats at a time, and would confer with the crews of the boats being led, to make it very clear that they all had to reach the beach at exactly the same time as the lead boat, with no exceptions. We all had our fins ready, so that if our boat was taken out, all of our surviving members would swim to another boat and one of those members would be swimming with the flag to attach it to a place on that boat.

Before I became a member of the Boat Unit, its shining hour had been during the Korean War on the major landing which was very successful in achieving perfect landings, way behind enemy lines. In that invasion, all of the boats carrying troops to the beach, unless they were destroyed coming in, lowered their ramps right on the beach and no one drowned. So it was very successful, however the fatalities were very high from the heavy fire.

When I joined the Assault Group, after the Korean War, we trained extensively with marines and with marine recon forces. Some training was done in Little Creek, and also Vieques, Puerto Rico. Those training sessions would often be a week to ten days, sometimes longer and we would be sleeping on the beach. The period I was in the Navy, from 1956 to 1961, was a very tense time, as one never knew when war might occur. At that time, Russia had atomic weapons, just as we had in the United States.

In our Unit we only traveled by ship. Admiral Howard Yeager was the one who realized that our Unit was now obsolete. There would probably be no more major beach landings and the fact that, unless we were on a ship nearby, it would take us ten days by ship to go to a place of conflict. So Yeager was the genius who created the Navy Seals, a unit that could parachute from a plane, jump from a helicopter, and that could be rapidly deployed within hours to anywhere in the world.

Two years after I left the Assault Group, when the Navy Seals unit was created, those in the Boat Unit and those in the UDT (Underwater Demolition Team) were given the choice of applying to become a Seal, which required six more months of training (and, I believe, having to extend their time in the service for three additional years) or to become a Swift Boat captain and crew in Vietnam. Senator John Kerry, Senator Robert Kerry and General Westmoreland's son (a Naval Academy graduate) chose to be Swift Boat members. In Vietnam the casualty rate for Swift Boat members was 8% a month (96% for a year).

I left the Assault Group in 1959 when I was selected to serve as a member of Admiral Brown's NATO staff. Admiral Brown was the Supreme Commander of Allied Forces Southern Europe. The headquarters was located in Naples, Italy and was considered the best duty in the Navy. My initial assignment was as a Communication Officer and as a NATO Diplomatic Courier. Then I was selected to serve as Assistant Cosmic Top Secret Control Officer – a very challenging position. I was probably selected on the recommendation of Admiral Howard Yeager, who had previously given me a letter of commendation when he was in charge of all Amphibious Forces on the east coast at that time. (Admiral Howard Yeager was outstanding in every way and I pray for him at Mass every Sunday.)

When Jane and I were married, I was on this assignment as Assistant Cosmic Top Secret Control Officer. I believe that it is the highest security clearance and information-handling service that exists. It is a stressful position. At that level you're dealing with information that is extremely secret and often deals with internal strategic information from the Russian satellite countries. One was not allowed to make the slightest mistake. On those messages, theoretically you're dealing with Presidents, or the Secretary of Defense in their NATO countries. But you never actually met any of these people. They would always have a person assigned to receive the message on their behalf. And with that person, even though you had seen the person ten times before, there was a very strict procedure you had to follow. You still had to see and verify their identification before giving them the information. You also retained a copy of that information back in Naples. I worked underground and so it was a very secure area where I was located. Many times the message would be the same to each of the various NATO countries, so there would be a number of flights to take, hopefully in the same day. Once that information had been delivered, I would return to Naples and go back to the NATO Headquarters.

I might mention I always flew on national airlines. For example, if I was flying to Ankara I would fly on a Turkish airline. The reason being that for taking messages, a civilian plane was much less likely to be shot down than a military plane. I would be armed and I would be the first one on the plane and the last one off the plane.

When I returned to Naples I would go to the underground tunnel and proceed to the Top Cosmic Control Room in the back of one of the tunnels that I controlled with the staff of two enlisted men. There we would have to dispose of our copy in a very clear way. In the procedure of the past, apparently many of the individuals in that position had taken our copy of the message to the Burn Center. There the message would be burned and you had to have two qualified individuals witness the burning. The ashes were then placed in water and flushed down the toilet. My understanding was that if one did the slightest thing wrong, he was immediately removed and sent back to the United States. Often they would be removed the same day that the mistake occurred. Thinking of the five officers before me who did not complete their tour, I still don't know the history of what happened to them. All I knew was that the five officers had not completed their tour, and since the various crypto machines had not been formally turned over, we had to develop an inventory of what had been used. Some crypto machines were used for days and some for as long as 30 days, but that would be rare for a cosmic top secret message. We would never use the same machine over again beyond those chosen dates, except when we were putting out a false message and hoping it would be decrypted by Russia. That was the only exception.

I decided that it was better to avoid going to the Burn Center so instead I asked for and received permission to burn them in our room in the tunnel. We're talking about a limited number of messages. We then burned them in the limited facilities that we had, with the qualified staff as witnesses, and properly disposed of them as required and properly signed our names as witnesses as required. I was never told what the previous five officers had done as far as making a mistake. It could have been as seemingly minor as not asking for identification from the person receiving the message in the NATO country. Even though we had seen the person ten times before, we were still required to review their identification. The job was very stressful and as a result, when I got home – winter, spring, summer, fall – Jane and I would always sit out on the balcony of our wonderful tiny villa, admiring the bay with a glass of wine, and then we would have dinner together.

Jane Elizabeth Scanlon

Envelope with Letter of Proposal to Marry

Joseph Alton Frisinger

26 February, 1960

My Dearest Jane,

I cannot live without you, my most precious love. I love you with all my heart and wish so much that I was with you now.

Jane, my most beautiful, wonderful girl that I love, will you marry me? Jane, I love you so and I promise that we will be happy. I will bring you flowers home and I will so love to take care of you. Please say "yes", for if you do I will be the happiest person in the world.

Spring has come to Naples and it is nice and sunny out. I am sure that you will love it here Jane - I know that I will if only we are together. Jane I have talked with the Catholic chaplain and there should be no trouble. I am to take a six course study and pass a test. I promise to you that we will go to the Catholic church together.

I love you with all my heart and I promise to make you happy - please marry me fine - please. I have been looking at apartments and have found one that will be perfect for you - it has a beautiful garden, a wonderful view and a th. + his wife live right below - it is a 2 apartment villa. The owner doesn't know whether he wants to rent it or sell it - but if he rents it I hope that it will be our first home. If we do get this, then we could get married in April - I wish that it were right now.

Please say "yes".

All my love,

Joe

Joe in Uniform

Cosmic Top Secret Clearance

Joe and Jane's Wedding, April 23, 1960

Joe and Jane's Wedding Party, April 23, 1960

Joe's parents Hubert and Gwen, Joe and Jane, and Jane's mother, Margaret

Jane and Joe cut the Cake

Jane sailing in Bermuda at the beginning of our honeymoon

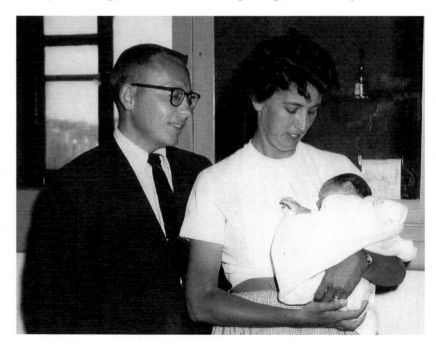

Linda Frisinger. The 2,500th baby born in an overseas Naval Hospital

Jane and baby Linda on the balcony of our villa in Naples, Italy

Easter Sunday. Linda, Jane and son Joe in front of our Ann Arbor home

Jane and children in the Roman Forum

Mike, Linda and Joe Jr.

Jane and children sailing on a Chinese Junk in the Bahamas

Joe and his brother Howard with their mother, Gwen

The children (singing) with Jane and her mother
at Villa San Michele, in Anacapri, Italy

SCHEDULE FOR OUR SUMMER TRIP - 1978

THURSDAY, JULY 27 TO THURSDAY, AUGUST 17

All DELTA AIRLINES

THURSDAY, JULY 27 San Diego to San Juan, Puerto Rico
                   Leave 7:00am arrive 8:13pm via New Orleans 920/964
FRIDAY,   JULY 28 In Puerto Rico
SATURDAY, JULY 29 In Puerto Rico
SUNDAY,   JULY 30 Fly to St. Thomas, Virgin Islands
MONDAY,   JULY 31 Sailing in Virgin Islands
TUESDAY,   AUGUST 1 St. Thomas to San Juan to New Orleans to Detroit
                   Leave San Juan at 11:35 flight 965 arrive in N.O. at 1:30pm
                   Leave New Orleans at 3:00pm arrive in Ann Arbor (Detroit)
                   at 7:29pm flight 762
WEDNESDAY, AUG. 2 In Ann Arbor
THURSDAY, AUG. 3 In Ann Arbor
FRIDAY,   AUG. 4 Detroit to Burlington, Vermont Leave at 9:24am and
                   arrive at 10:40am on flight 858.
SATURDAY, AUG. 5 Burlington, Vermont to Boston to Bermuda
                   Leave Burlington at 7:50am and arrive in Bermuda at 12:05pm
                   flights 706/1161
SUNDAY,   AUG. 6 In Bermuda
MONDAY,   AUG. 7 In Bermuda
TUESDAY,   AUG. 8 Leave Bermuda at 4:25pm to Boston arriving at 5:22pm
                   flight 1162
WEDNESDAY, AUG. 9 In Newport, Rhode Island
THURSDAY, AUG. 10 In Newport
FRIDAY,   AUG. 11 In Newport
SATURDAY, AUG. 12 BOSTON to Denver Leave Boston at 1:46pm through Atlanta
                   and arrive in Denver at 5:05pm flights 741/555
SUNDAY,   AUG. 13 At Mom's in Fort Collins, Colorado
MONDAY,   AUG. 14 At Mom's in Fort Collins
TUESDAY,   Aug. 15 At Mom's in Fort Collins
Wednesday AUG. 16 At Mom's in Fort Collins
THURSDAY, AUG. 17 Denver to San Diego via Atlanta. We leave Denver at 9:30am
                   and arrive in Atlanta at 1:56pm flight 504. We leave
                   Atlanta at 4:20pm and arrive in San Diego at 7:08pm
                   flight 1025.

HOPE EVERY ONE HAS A GOOD TIME

Our wonderful Twenty-One Days of Travel on Delta for $199 in 1978

Sailing with Jane at the wheel

Sailing with Joe at the wheel

Sailing with Linda at the wheel

Sailing with Mike at the wheel

Sailing with our wonderful niece Cindy (yellow polo shirt)
and Joe Jr. at the wheel

Joe Jr., Cindy, Linda, and Mike. Boys in coat and tie, girls in long dresses –
the required dinner dress in Bermuda

A wonderful picture of Jane with her brother, Bob Scanlon,
their mother, Margaret, and Bob's wife, Kay, in 1980

Linda graduating from the University of Santa Clara

Our home in La Jolla, also showing the little cabin on the hill

This is the living room area in our La Jolla home

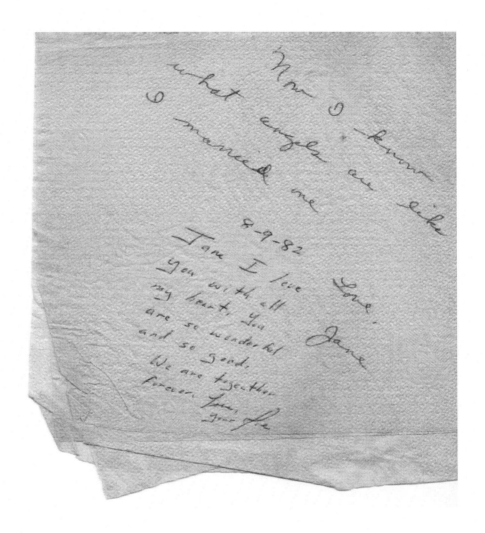

There would be a love note like this in my lunch pail each day

Shannon and Joe Jr.'s Wedding

My brother Howard (a Catholic Deacon) conducting the Wedding of
Shannon and Joe Jr. in All Hallows Parish in La Jolla

Group of six on the canal boat Mistral in Friesland

Shannon and Joe Jr.'s family – Nick, Cody and Shane and the dogs

Jane and grandson Shane after picking oranges

Jane and Joe with Priest in Bermuda

Linda, Janet (Jane's niece) and Jane at a side patio of our home in La Jolla

Jane and Joe's 50th Wedding Anniversary

Jane and Joe's 54th
Wedding Anniversary
April 23, 2014

JANE and JOE FRISINGER
6875 Via Valverde, La Jolla, CA 920377 (858) 459-0356
Email: jfrisi2747@aol.com

May 25, 2007

Dear Joe,
       Thank you for such a
wonderful vacation to Kauai. You
always pick a beautiful location,
and this is Tops. It is so
peaceful and the mountains so
beautiful. Happy Birthday,
              Love, Jane

Our home in Princeville – Hawaii State Flag flying in front

This is the dining room and living room in our Princeville home

My brother Howard and his wife Mim with Jane and me in our home
in Princeville, Kauai

Neighbors in Princeville singing Christmas Carols for Jane

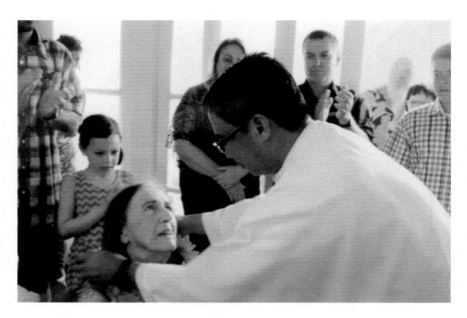

Our Pastor, Father Ramelo placing a beautiful Flower Lei on Jane and praying for her in April, 2014

Family visitation with Jane at the Taunton, Mass. funeral home

13. MY GUARDIAN ANGEL

There are many people who believe in Guardian Angels, and there are many who do not believe in Guardian Angels. In the case of Jane and me, we believe that we have a Guardian Angel. In my life I have been saved six times from certain death by my Guardian Angel, and also, my Guardian Angel has spoken to me.

Some of the others who believe there are Guardian Angels include Richard Dreyfuss, the famous actor. In *The Week* interview, Richard Dreyfuss described a 1982 incident. He said he was a terrible person, sleeping with other people's wives, on drugs, on alcohol, and openly criticizing others. One night he was at a producer's home for dinner and he ended the evening by screaming obscenities at his hostess. He then got into his two-passenger Mercedes sports car and he took off at high speed. The next thing he remembers, he was upside down in a tree, and his seat belt was on. He said, "I have never put on a seat belt in my life and yet there I was hanging upside down and saved from death from having my seat belt on." He then felt like his life was saved by a Guardian Angel. And he said it completely changed his entire life. Instead of being a terrible person, he changed and wanted to be the best person he could ever be. At the end of the interview the last words he said were, "I did not put my seat belt on."

So there are others who believe in Guardian Angels.

Six times, I believe my life was saved by my Guardian Angel, starting when I was fourteen years old. During the summer when I was fourteen, I would take care of a number of neighbors' yards with a traditional push mower. On a particular evening I had already completed the mowing, weeding and trimming of three neighbors' yards and I was tired. But I did want to go out horseback riding as I had planned to do that evening while it was still light. As it turned out, I went with four other people, two of them young men going to the University of Michigan, and two young women, probably their dates. At about 8:30pm, when it was still light, they decided to stop and get off the horses to take a rest. When we were ready to get back on our horses, for some crazy reason I started to get on my horse on the right side instead of the left side. And I don't know why. I had been riding horses since I was seven years old but through over-tiredness or whatever, I made a serious mistake. The horse threw me and as I was lying on the ground, the horse rose up and his front hoofs were coming down straight toward my head. At that instant one of the men dove off his horse, hit the shoulder of my horse and landed on top of me, and the hoof went right by my ear. He had saved my life. Our saddles were Western with the pommel in front. If anyone had asked me if someone could dive from a western saddle, I would say it was almost impossible. But in this case the impossible was possible and he saved my life.

The second time that my life was saved was when I was sixteen and I'd told my parents I was taking three fellow student guys with me to go to the Ann Arbor High School football team game. I did not tell my parents that the game was in East Lansing, almost sixty miles away. After the game was over, we were driving back on the two-lane road and I was going 100 mph. Way ahead of us, a farmer's tractor pulling a wagon drove onto the road. I put on the brakes and tried to slow down as quickly as I could. As I was reaching him, I went onto the shoulder of the road and the car went over. Amazingly, none of us was hurt, not even a scratch. This was before seat belts and air bags. We got out of the car and with the power of adrenalin, we were able to lift the car off its side and, at least for a short time, it was almost drivable. The farmer did not stop to see how we were doing. As we drove the car away with one side caved in, we did not think to check to see if we had lost water when the car went over. And apparently it had. After a few miles, the car stopped.

The third time that my life was saved was when I was an employee with the City of Ann Arbor after I got out of the Navy. This was in the mid-1960s. The University of Michigan Hospital was one of four hospitals in the nation that started to perform open heart surgery. The medical team felt that all precautions should be taken and as a result they felt the blood given by donors should be as fresh as possible. That meant having volunteers give blood the evening before surgery scheduled for the next morning. The method of taking the blood was also unique. Instead of taking blood through normal blood flow, they decided to take it by pumping it out and that way the blood would be fresher. This meant that the blood could be taken out in a period of five minutes versus the normal twenty minutes. The procedure was potentially dangerous because there could be a malfunction of the pump and it could lead to drawing blood out much more quickly than anticipated. As a result, the requirement was that the nurse had to be sitting beside the machine during the entire time the blood was being drawn. Two times previously I had been a volunteer giving blood, and there was no problem. The rule was absolute that the nurse must stay in the room until the necessary blood was completely withdrawn.

In my case, the nurse had left the room and the machine went crazy and was drawing blood at an extremely high rate, resulting in my heart being emptied of blood and in fibrillation. By that time I was unconscious and apparently the nurse had returned and had called the code blue. While unconscious, I heard a doctor say, "I think we're losing him." But somehow I made it through and they replaced some of my blood and had me stay there for a number of hours under observation before allowing me to go home. Soon afterwards, that method of drawing blood was eliminated by all four hospitals.

The fourth time that my life was saved was in 1994 while in San Diego working at Mercy Hospital Medical Center. I would always go in early and then I would go down to our small boat, the 23-foot Ranger. I would change clothes and put on my Navy fins and go for a mile and a half swim. Then I would have lunch. I used the same lunch pail as I had during summer breaks while in college working highway construction. Jane always prepared my lunch with the same ingredients. I had a thermos of milk, a peanut butter and jelly sandwich, an apple and she always included a love note.

One particular day, instead of going swimming, we were using our work boat to move boats into different slips. The work boat had about three inches of growth on the bottom. It was an older wooden boat, about 14 feet in length. After moving the boats, I said, "I'm going to take the work boat near my boat and I'm going to clean off the bottom. I think I have a big spade in my dock box." I found that I did not have a big spade. Rather, I had a four-inch putty knife. So I thought, "This is going to take a long time." I stayed in the water, diving and scraping, firstly taking off all the grass that was on the bottom of the boat and then scraping off all of the coral attached to the bottom of the boat. So dive after dive after dive. Two hours later I had completed the job and in the process I had about fifty small cuts from the coral on both of my arms. About four days later I noticed that I was gaining weight. And I've never gained weight! Then I began to get a headache that became pretty extreme.

At that time, our Catholic Bishop for San Diego had been down in Mexico and when stepping off a curb he felt extreme head pain. It was diagnosed as a tumor in his brain, which was cancer, Stage 4. He died soon afterward.

Stepping off a curb for me at that point was extremely painful, and I was beginning to lose vision. I thought I might be getting a brain tumor. So I called a close friend who was an oncologist and described to him my symptoms. He knew that I swam at least four times a week, so he asked me if I had any cuts from coral. I said I had. He asked where I had been swimming. I told him I had been swimming in the water inside Shelter Island where a few of the boats that were docked would illegally empty their holding tanks into the water. So the water was often quite contaminated. By that time my vision was going and later, the only things I could see were white dots.

My oncologist friend said, "Joe, you don't have a brain tumor, you have viral encephalitis. That's caused by the coral that develops in contaminated water. Frankly, Joe there's nothing we can do. There's no treatment for it with the exception of opening up the skull, and that rarely works. You have a 50/50 chance of living and you're going to be in a very deep unconscious state for 72 hours, or less, if you pass away. So if things work out for you, after 72 hours the body will have fought off the virus to the point where you see the white dots again. Then you'll slowly be able to recover your sight and your ability to think." He added, "The options you have are that we can admit you to the hospital, or you can stay at home in a very dark room, and Jane will take care of you, giving sips of water, that type of thing. That would be your best option. Complete darkness is essential so there is no stimulation of the brain due to light." Jane told the doctor, "I will take care of him at home." And the doctor replied, "Jane, I will call you five times during each day, and you can call me any time day or night if you need help, or if Joe is going into seizures and you feel uncomfortable having him at home."

Luckily, after 72 hours, I started to see light flashes. By the end of three weeks I was ready to return to continuing my life. When I went back to church (where I was an usher) people asked, "Where have you been?" And I told them I'd had viral encephalitis, and "Now I'm fine." Each of them responded, "I knew someone who had viral encephalitis, but of course he died." It took me more than six months before I could step off a curb without severe head pain. I had to be very mindful.

The fifth time my Guardian Angel saved my life was less dramatic. It was in March or April of 1997 and it happened at Silver Gate Yacht Club on Shelter Island in San Diego, California. I was going down the main dock when I noticed that one of the sailboats had apparently taken on water, as it was much lower in the water than normal. As I was passing by, I thought that I would go back to the Club House to call the owner and then come back to the boat and go aboard. For some reason, however, I felt that if I was going aboard – go aboard now.

So I went aboard and found that the water level in the cabin was at least fifteen inches above the cabin floor. The boat had a connection to the Club's main water line and I discovered that there was a break in the boat's connection, and water was pouring into the boat. I turned off the internal valve for the incoming water. As I was preparing to get off the boat,

I noticed that there was a regular home-type electrical outlet on the wall of the boat's cabin, and the water level appeared to be less than a quarter of an inch below it, soon to enter that outlet. I realized then that if I had spent the ten or fifteen minutes it would have taken me to call the owner, by the time I returned and stepped into the flooded boat, I would have been electrocuted. So I immediately got off the boat and unplugged the electrical cord from the dock's power box. I then went up to the Club House, and called the owner of the boat. Then two members went down with me to the boat with the Club's pump and we pumped out the water.

Our small (23-foot long) sailboat did not have an electrical connection, so I hadn't even thought about that when I stepped into the boat.

The sixth time my life was saved was during an adventure in Europe. Jane and I had chartered a three-cabin canal boat in the beautiful small town of Sneek in Freisland (now part of the Netherlands) on the North Sea. We asked two other couples to go with us. I was the only one of the six of us who had experience in small power boats. And so I was the one who checked out the boat where they had me take it out and perform different things. Everything went well. I asked, "What is the maximum speed on the canals?" They said it was five knots. And I asked them, "What is that in engine revolutions so I will know the exact number?" And they gave me the number. While 90% of our time would be spent in canals, during the first day we were going across a very large lake, almost an inland sea. On the lake there were buoys set up, just like a runway, with the 60-foot-wide lane extending across the whole lake. Each boat crossing the lake was to stay within this lane.

Since I had the experience in various power boats, we mutually decided that each of the husbands could stand a two-hour watch. There were two steering stations on the boat, one on deck and one in the main cabin. I would always serve my watches up on deck. The other two men preferred to serve some of their watches in the main cabin where they had full visibility ahead just as above, though not in back.

While we were going across the lake, we were all down in the main cabin going at exactly five knots through the 60-foot-wide marked lane. All of a sudden, my Guardian Angel said very clearly to me, "Get up on deck." I went right up on deck and saw that directly in back of us was a 40-foot wide, 120-foot long barge that was fully loaded to the point where the tug boat pushing it could not see over the pile on the barge, which likely weighed about 100 tons. It was clearly gaining on us.

I ran down to the cabin, put the throttle on full and pulled the wheel all the way over to the right. We escaped by about one minute. If I had not responded to my Guardian Angel's message, there would have been a small bump and we would have disintegrated from the impact. There is no possible way I could have heard that coming. Tug boats are extremely quiet because their blades are so large and turn so slowly. And in the main cabin we were right over our own engine. So even if the tug boat had made noise we would not have heard it. On that day, my Guardian Angel saved six lives. *We later learned that on the lake the maximum speed is seven knots.*

In addition to the six times my Guardian Angel saved my life, my Guardian Angel also saved my mother's life.

One Saturday morning as I was waking up, my Guardian Angel said, "Your mother's in trouble." As plain as hearing a friend's voice. I was in La Jolla and my mother was 600 miles away in Fort Collins, Colorado.

I immediately called the home of my brother and sister-in-law. My brother was down in Denver for a meeting, and my sister-in-law was at home. I told her, "Please go and check on mom right away. I think she's in trouble." When my sister-in-law went directly up and found that my mother had overdosed on barbital, she immediately called 911.

An ambulance rushed my mother to the hospital, pumped out her stomach, gave her treatment and she survived. I flew out right away and Jane followed the next day. I knew my mother had been feeling sad and stressed. She was finding that taking care of the house and the very big yard that she had was becoming more and more difficult. My brother had suggested having someone come in to help her a few days a week. That would not work out for her. Things were not where she thought they should be, and she did not want anyone to come anymore. I knew she was depressed.

The hospital required that a family member be with the patient 24 hours a day in their room. I took the 8pm – 8am shift. Others filled in the day period. After mom was released from the hospital, her life changed for the better. She fell deeply in love with a man from the church who we all thought was tremendous. He would visit her every day and life became much better for her. Eight years later, she died peacefully in a retirement facility with this wonderful person coming over to take her out for lunch or dinner almost every day. They were truly in love.

So this was another example of listening to my Guardian Angel, and how I was able to facilitate my mother having a rewarding final stretch of her life.

14. FROM LA JOLLA TO KAUAI
AND LIFE IN PRINCEVILLE

During the forty years we lived in La Jolla the natural beauty remained the same but, over those forty years, La Jolla became one of the most sought-after communities in the United States. Its population doubled and housing prices zoomed up steeply. People from around the world both visited La Jolla and purchased homes in La Jolla. As you might expect, the "feed" stores were the first to go and then the Plymouth and Chevrolet dealers were next. Then the family-type restaurants were changed into very upscale restaurants. The car dealers became Rolls Royce, Bentley, Bugatti (at 3.5 million), plus many of the European sport cars. La Jolla had been transformed into one of the world's most beautiful international communities. However, it still remained a wonderful place to live and our street – Via Valverde – basically remained the same.

The great increase in home prices allowed Jane and me to think of other places to live. By then our children were living in different parts of the country. Our daughter, Linda, was living in Raleigh, North Carolina. Our son, Joe Jr. and his family were living in Benicia in northern California, and our son Michael was living in Scottsdale, Arizona. After our children had grown up, Jane and I would take a trip to Europe (including Ireland) each year – usually with two other couples. From 1999 to 2007 we would also take a trip to Kauai and stay – with two other couples – in the beautiful North Shore village of Princeville where we would rent a three-bedroom condo for eight nights. We would always rent a van and Jane and I would enjoy showing the other couples the many beautiful sights of Kauai. At the condo I would get up at 5:30am each morning and go for a ninety-minute walk. After that I would stop at the Foodland grocery store to buy pastries and then have coffee on when Jane and our four friends were ready for breakfast at 7:30 or 8am. During those walks I covered every street in Princeville and quickly concluded that we wanted to live on Aloalii Drive which had beautiful homes on large lots with wonderful ocean and mountain views. In taking Jane to that street, she agreed and felt it was perfect.

Following our 2007 trip to Kauai, both Jane and I decided that of all of the places we had visited in the world, Kauai (especially the North Shore) was the most beautiful place in the world and we decided that Princeville was the place where we wanted to live. The island of Kauai has only 70,000 residents and they are scattered among two towns – Lihue and Kapa'a – and about thirteen villages. The North Shore is the most lush (meaning it gets the most rain and everything is green and the jungles are dense) part in all of the Hawaiian Islands. Hanalei Bay is also considered the most scenic bay in all of Hawaii. The North Shore has many one-lane bridges (somewhat like "old Hawaii") which we treasure. And Kauai has a building height requirement that no building can be higher than 30 feet in height (although sometimes they allow 32 or 33 feet) so NO HIGH RISES.

In 2008 we put our La Jolla home on the market for sale. The timing was not great as this was the beginning of the recession and home prices were falling rapidly. We kept lowering the price of our home to "the market value" but no homes were selling at "the market value" so we kept going lower. In March of 2010 we finally sold our home and we arranged with the buyers (a wonderful family) to rent it from them for two months as we were having our 50th wedding anniversary party in April. That was fine with the buyers as they were currently renting a home in La Jolla and their rental contract ended in June. Our home sold for twenty times what we had paid for it in 1970 and the ongoing recession also affected the prices of houses on Kauai, so we did very well. After the closing of the sale of our La Jolla home, I called our realtor in Princeville and told him what we could pay for the home we wanted to buy on Aloalii Drive. He replied "Joe, the only chance you have to buy it at that price is all cash and a 15-day escrow." I said, "Fine." Our realtor made the offer and the owners accepted it. We had just purchased our dream home and we named our new home SEAFAIR. Our home in La Jolla was named SEAGULL HAVEN.

During the two months from the time our La Jolla home was sold to the time we would be leaving, we told the wonderful family (including three children) who had purchased our home that we planned to have all of the neighbors over for them to "meet you and welcome you and for your children to meet the children in the neighborhood."

In checking with our neighbors, they said the best time would be on a Sunday afternoon, since many of the children were involved with soccer on Saturdays.

This invitation – to have a party for the family – was made after our 50th anniversary celebration, and six weeks before our actual departure date. The husband is the Director of Replacement Surgery for the University of California Hospital in La Jolla. He is a specialist in liver transplant surgery, which is considered to be the hardest and most challenging transplant of all. So, he is a very talented person. Since he was often scheduled for surgery, the party ended up being on the final Sunday before our departure.

We had a total of 52 neighbors and their children over that Sunday afternoon and the wife (Marie) and children were present and able to meet their new neighbors and especially the children in the neighborhood. The house looked great for the party, including the yard and we had a number of tables outside. The party was a great success, and everyone had time to visit with their neighbors and to welcome the incoming family.

At the party the neighbors with children had prepared a beautiful work of art with each child having painted a fish, or a sea shell, or – in the case of the six-month old baby – a foot print. Jane and I were overwhelmed, especially since they also presented us with a video of the children creating the artwork. We said that this picture was the first one that we would put up in our new home, and it was.

The following day, Monday, our cars were picked up (Jane's 1994 Camry and my 2005 Corolla). Our wonderful neighbor, Fred Binks helped us take a number of things to a holding area for the Sisters of Mercy down in Tijuana that same day, using his car.

On Tuesday the packers came and it was a whirlwind of a day. They were packing everything. Our daughter-in-law had forewarned us to make sure to not have any garbage in the house. She said, "If you do, you'll find it packed and going with all your other household goods." As they were packing things, Jane and I noticed items probably brought from our Ann Arbor home forty years earlier, that we could never remember having, and we would ask each other, "Where did that come from?" In addition to the furniture, we had 96 boxes, many weighing 70 pounds each.

The shipping container came on Wednesday. It was packed and on its way to the island of Kauai by 3pm that day. It was not to be seen again by Jane and me until it arrived in port six weeks later.

Our flight safely landed in Lihue, Kauai on May 13, 2010 and we were both exhausted when we arrived. We had had very little sleep for the previous three nights because of the process of moving. As described, our cars were picked up on Monday, our packers came on Tuesday and the container arrived to be filled on Wednesday.

It was early evening when we arrived on Kauai. We rented a car and asked for directions to Wal-Mart in order to buy one cot (for Jane), two sleeping bags, two face cloths and a few other items to take these things to our new home. The directions that were given to us by the car rental company in terms of getting to Wal-Mart were crystal clear. He indicated it was only a five-minute drive away.

For some reason, I got lost, stopped at two gas stations in Lihue and finally got to Wal-Mart after 45 minutes. In Wal-Mart we purchased the needed items. We then drove, with our number of bags, toward Princeville. After driving half of the way to Princeville, I pulled over to count the bags again. I discovered we were one bag short, and that bag contained the cameras and some other equipment. So I turned around, went back to and parked at the airport, took the parking slip and walked into the airport. I asked where the Lost and Found was located. I was directed to the very east end of the terminal.

As I was walking quickly down the corridor to the Lost and Found, I apparently dropped the parking slip. When I found the Lost and Found, the woman was tremendous. She said, "I think you're looking for a bag, aren't you?" And I said, "Yes." And she said, "Here it is." And I thought how wonderful they are, I was very impressed. As I was going back to the car, I realized that I had lost the parking slip. If this happened at the San Diego airport, you might be paying the maximum charge for perhaps a week's parking time. Once I had returned to Jane and our rental car, I drove over, parked on the side of the exit, and waited until there was a break in the stream of cars going through the exit gate. Then I walked up to the person in the booth. The attendant said, "I think you're going to tell me you can't find your parking slip." And I said, "Yes." She said, "A person at the United Airlines counter saw you walking quickly and saw you drop your slip. He left the counter and picked up the slip. He had lost sight of you, so he brought it to me and described you as the person who lost it." I was so impressed with them doing this, and by the welcoming spirit they had.

When we reached Princeville, I did not have the code for the gate, so we waited until a car came along and we followed that car in, and drove down our street. Once there, we parked in the driveway of our new home. Our realtor had told us that the owners of the house across the street had the key to our house, and to just knock on their door. So I knocked on the door of the house that was sort of directly across from our house. It was 9:15pm and they were already asleep, but the husband came to the door. I explained who I was, and he said, "You want the person next door, they are expecting you. He is also a realtor in the same firm as your realtor." When we knocked on that door, the person gave us a wonderful welcome and was so glad we were there. Soon after, upon opening the door of our new home, we found that he had left all kinds of things for our breakfast the next morning, which was very kind. When we turned on the lights in our home, however, and looked at the living and dining room area, my initial impression was, "We have bought a garage." The back walls of the house are virtually all glass, and all of the blinds were down, covering the windows, and the house was empty of furniture. This made it appear like numerous garage doors.

The next morning I put up all the blinds, and they have never been down since, for the views are breathtaking. The next morning the neighbor came over – from the home where I had first knocked – with a bottle of wine and welcomed us. While we were talking, I learned that he was in the Naval Assault Group based in Coronado, California, whereas I was with the Assault Group in Little Creek, Virginia. He was UDT (Underwater Demolition Team) and had many dangerous missions during the Korean War, including missions in back of enemy lines. So we had an instant bonding, with both of us being in the Assault Groups. Rod and his wife, Frances would become our best friends here in Princeville. He noticed we had no furniture or kitchenware and a half-hour later he appeared at our front door with a huge tray which was filled with dishes, silverware and pots and pans. On that weekend our next door neighbors Bill and Mary had us over for a cook-out and to meet other neighbors. A great welcome!

Six weeks later our furniture and 96 boxes of things from our La Jolla home arrived. I had the delivery crew put the 96 boxes in the large entry hall, knowing that being there, I would have to go through them, because if I had them put in the garage they might still be there. We did unpack 92 of those boxes and decided to put the remaining four boxes in the garage. We labeled them "surprise boxes" that we would open later. We still have not opened them.

Throughout our marriage, Jane was truly a genius in financial management. This was true in Naples, Italy, in Toledo, Ohio, in Ann Arbor, Michigan, in La Jolla, California and also in Princeville on Kauai, the Garden Island of Hawaii.

Jane made sure that every possible dollar that could be saved, was saved. This was especially true in Toledo where my salary was twice what I was making in the Navy. All of that was saved. In Ann Arbor when we were involved in developing chartered trips to Bermuda, the Bahamas and Europe, all of that income was saved too.

As a result of our savings, we were able to purchase attractive homes in Ann Arbor, La Jolla, and in Princeville, Kauai. In terms of weekly and monthly budgets, Jane had the envelope system. There was an envelope for church, an envelope for food, an envelope for gas for the cars, and an envelope for entertainment. The bills such as electricity and water were all paid through money in our checking account. Jane wrote all the checks. In the checking account Jane's calculation was never different from the bank statement, by even a penny. Now, I am lucky to be even as close as $70 to the bank statement. So I change my figure to match the bank's figure.

In terms of entertaining, Jane was magnificent. She enjoyed having people over and she would say, "We can have eight people over for wine and cheese for less than the cost of the two of us going out for dinner." As a result, we had a lot of people over for wine and cheese and we hardly ever went out for dinner. This practice continued in Princeville and we would have sometimes as many as 22 people over for wine and cheese to celebrate a special event, such as a birthday or new neighbors arriving, or existing neighbors leaving.

In Princeville this tradition even continued when Jane was in a wheelchair and unable to remember names of our visitors. I would set up the living room with Jane in her wheelchair right in front of the fireplace, with a chair on each side of her. All of our neighbors and friends knew what that meant. When they came over, they would each give Jane a hug and thank her for inviting them. Also, the chairs next to her were almost always filled. If there was an empty chair for a few minutes, I would go and sit with Jane until the next person asked to sit with her. They all understood not to ask Jane a question because they knew she would not be able to answer it. So they thanked her for the party, told her what they were doing, what was new in their lives. Many would often remark that it was so wonderful that Jane was from beautiful Newport, Rhode Island, and Jane sometimes remembered that she grew up in Newport. At the end of the party, every person would go to Jane, give her another hug (the human touch is so important even to those whose memory is fading or gone) and thank her for inviting them to the party. Jane was treated as the hostess, which she was.

In April of 2014 Jane suddenly had a very lucid moment. She told me, "Joe, I want you to know that I'm ready to go." For a period of about 15 minutes Jane was completely lucid and seemed to remember everything about our life together and how much she loved me. After those 15 minutes Jane's memory quickly faded. Those 15 minutes were and still are very precious to me. In telling my sister-in-law Mim about those 15 minutes, Mim, who had been a nurse and then a hospice nurse, told me that sometimes Alzheimer's patients have those brief lucid moments, especially when they are talking with the one whom they love.

Our first caregiver told us that she always slept in the same room as the person for whom she was caring. Each caregiver continued that plan and slept in Jane's bedroom.

In December of 2013, I asked the caregiver to sleep in the upstairs guest room, because I wanted to be sleeping in Jane's room. Any visitors would sleep in the spacious upstairs master bedroom.

Jane often did not recognize me and as a result it would be uncomfortable for her to have someone who she did not know sleeping next to her in bed. As a result, I slept on the floor next to her bed from December 2013 until her death in June 2014, and I continued to sleep on the floor in her room for the two months following her passing.

In way of background, sleeping on the floor was nothing new to me, as I had often done that on many of our trips to Europe. I would sleep on the floor because I cannot sit on a couch or regular living room chair.

The reason for this is that while back on base in the Navy when I was with the Assault Group, I would almost always complete the obstacle course in the evening just to keep in good condition. That seemed to never be a problem except for one time when I was returning from a three-month assignment that did not require strenuous exercise.

The evening I returned to Little Creek from that assignment, I went over to do the obstacle course. This was 1958 in early April (but the ground was still frozen with some snow on the ground). I completed all of the obstacles except for one. The last obstacle was the High Line which was a 60-foot long rope that I would pull myself across, twelve feet off the ground. In the middle of attempting to complete the High Line, I was so exhausted that I fell and landed on my back.

Three days later I went on a mission and things seemed to be going all right. On the mission I developed paralysis on my right lower side and coming back from the mission, my right leg seemed to be paralyzed. Going up the ship's ladders from one level to another I would pull myself up. When I got back to base I was immediately placed in the Naval Hospital in Norfolk.

Their x-rays showed injury to my spine resulting in the paralysis on my right side. I was scheduled for surgery on Wednesday as a neurosurgeon came down from Bethesda Naval Hospital (where President Reagan was taken when he was shot many years later) in the Washington DC area. Tuesday evening two sailors were in an auto accident and required brain surgery. As a result, my surgery was delayed until a week later.

Meanwhile, on the following day, Thursday, one of the corpsman said,

"You're a member of the team, and we have a swimming pool here. It's not warm, it's about 55-58 degrees, but I can take you down there." Then the corpsman took me down to the pool. With my hands I could pull myself through the water, and I began to get feeling back in my right leg. The corpsman continued to take me down to the pool, now three times a day for the next five days. By then I was getting motion on my right side and it seemed to be getting better each day.

The doctors ordered a new x-ray and found that as I strengthened my back muscles, my spine was becoming better and perhaps would not require surgery after all. In releasing me, the doctor said, "To maintain this recovery, you are going to have to do many strenuous exercises for the rest of your life, because the muscles in your back are keeping this portion of the spine in place."

Upon release, I was still with the Assault Group, but was basically serving as one of the instructors. Gradually I was able to complete the obstacle course again on my own and I have continued to do strenuous exercises for the rest of my life ever since.

Currently, I get up in the morning, have a cup of coffee, do 200 push-ups, go for a fast bike ride followed by another 200 push-ups, and that is how I start each day. The ongoing situation, though, is that I cannot sit on a soft chair, or sleep on a soft mattress. So I have a favorite hard wooden chair and a very firm mattress.

This explains why I had no problem sleeping on the floor in Jane's room and I would often sleep on the floor during our vacations in Europe.

15. JANE AND ALZHEIMER'S

Alzheimer's is a disease that gradually sneaks up on you. Some people notice that a friend is showing signs of Alzheimer's Disease before others notice. This was especially true in my case.

I was told many years later that during the last few years that Jane and I lived in La Jolla, that some of our neighbors and some of the people at church thought Jane was developing Alzheimer's Disease. I did not notice that at all. And there were many times when I should have noticed it.

For example, we would go to the doctor for Jane's yearly check-up. The doctor was a friend of mine, on the staff at Mercy Hospital, so I knew him very well. The doctor would ask Jane a question and Jane would turn to me and I would answer for her. I didn't think anything of that. I thought that Jane realized that I was a friend of the doctor's and that I could provide the answer more clearly than she could.

Also in terms of things like shopping, Jane was very independent and would do shopping on her own but during the last few years in La Jolla, she would often say, when we were coming back from sailing, "Could we stop at Ralph's to do some shopping?" That was unusual, because Jane in the past had always done shopping on her own. But Ralph's was right on our way home from the yacht club and again, I did not think anything about that. This continued through our move to Kauai.

We sold our house in La Jolla in March 2010 and then rented it back for two months as we were planning to celebrate our 50th wedding anniversary on April 23 and the invitations to attend had already gone out to family and friends. This was one of our biggest events of our married life and we held the celebration dinner at the Silver Gate Yacht Club, where we had been members since 1970. We had a fabulous dinner, with wine and 52 attending including, of course, our children and Shannon, the wife of our oldest son, Joe and their three sons. My brother Howard and sister-in-law Mim were also part of this family celebration. It was a great evening.

With Jane, things appeared as normal as ever to me and, after moving to Kauai, since we were new to the Island, Jane and I would always go out together to shop. Four weeks after our arrival in Kauai, our two cars, Jane's 1994 Camry and my 2005 Corolla arrived in the port and we went down to pick them up. We turned in our rental car and then we drove the two cars back to our home in Princeville. Jane was following me and she was driving sometimes a little over the line but really doing well. We were going slowly.

The next morning after we were home, Jane said she had lost her Driver's License. She had all of her other cards, but she couldn't find her Driver's License. I thought, well, Jane is very smart and she has always been much smarter than I am. I assumed that Jane felt uncomfortable driving in a new, strange place and I thought she was very wise in saying she had lost her Driver's License, rather than saying that she did not feel comfortable driving. Instead of being alerted to a problem, I was impressed by her great judgment. I have to admit that I was impressed with everything Jane did.

Each year, Jane and I would go to Europe and we would always stay in very inexpensive places or take a cruise. In October of 2010, this time leaving from our new home base of Kauai, we went to Europe and took an ocean cruise from Venice, going to Greece and then to Turkey. In Turkey, our shore visits included going to Ephesus in Turkey where Mary, the mother of Jesus lived her final years.

When we returned to Kauai we had a check-up with the physician we had chosen here on the Island. She suggested that I make an appointment with a neurologist to talk with both of us, especially Jane. I really did not know why, but I did make this appointment with the neurologist that she recommended. When we met with the neurologist, he asked Jane a number of questions, such as, "What year is it?" and "Who is the President?" She was unable to answer any of the questions that he asked, and he indicated the diagnosis was Alzheimer's Disease. Jane accepted the diagnosis and I felt extremely surprised and sad. I realized then why the doctor had recommended we see a neurologist, for us to be given the diagnosis of Alzheimer's Disease more officially.

Jane advised me early on in her Alzheimer's that she wanted to be buried beside her mother and father in the St. Francis Cemetery in Taunton, Massachusetts. The plot is the Scanlon plot, and when Jane's mother died in 1986, it was technically already filled, but the Superintendent in charge of the cemetery said they would make an exception for Jane's mother. So Jane's mother, Margaret was buried beside her husband, Edward.

Knowing that Jane's wish was to be buried next to her parents, in early February of 2012, I called the cemetery office and talked with the Secretary, and asked if they could make another exception, for Jane. The Secretary said, "I'll check with the Superintendent." When she called back she said, "We did make an exception for Jane's mother and we've never made a second exception." Two weeks later I called again. She said, "Well, I'll ask him again." I pointed out how important it was to Jane. She called back and said, "The Superintendent has said we've never made a second exception."

At the end of the month I called a third time and again pointed out how important it was to Jane, and how wonderful Jane was, and could they possibly make a second exception. The Secretary said, "I'll ask him, perhaps we're wearing him down." A few days later the Secretary called back and said, "Yes, the Superintendent will make a second exception and Jane will be buried next to her mother's grave." How very wonderful are the Secretary and Superintendent.

In March of each year I would always have a birthday party basically for Jane but also for neighbors who have their birthdays in March. In March 2012 we had the party and it was a wonderful celebration and perfect for Jane and the others. A large neighborhood get-together and party.

The Friday following the party, as I was helping Jane get into bed, she fell. At that time I was not strong enough to lift Jane up and into bed. So a neighbor came over and even though together we could have put Jane into bed, he thought it was prudent to have the firefighters come over and do an assessment. So for the moment we made sure she was comfortable on the floor while we called and waited for assistance. When the firefighters arrived, one of them was a paramedic and she did a complete examination of Jane. She said, "I think Jane is fine. We can have her transported to hospital if you like, but I think she is fine." I agreed and two of the firefighters picked Jane up and gently put her into bed. Perfect.

The next morning Jane was able to get up by herself and the day was a normal day. That night as she was getting to bed, I should have been much more alert, as she fell again. At that point, about 9pm, I went and looked outside and all the lights in the neighbors' homes were out. And so I said, "Jane we're going to have a night together on the floor and we'll be very comfortable with blankets and pillows and you'll feel much better tomorrow."

The next day Jane was able to get up with my help, and the day proceeded normally and I stayed home all day with her. On the third night, when Jane fell again, I wondered, what was I thinking? Luckily, she wasn't hurt. A neighbor was able to come over and help me get her into bed.

The next day I called a very close friend in the canoe club and he came over three times each day to help with Jane, and each evening his wife came over to help with Jane. What wonderful friends. By that time I had a wheelchair and I was able to get Jane from the wheelchair to the bed without any problem. It's easier to pick someone up when they are already half-way up rather than from being on the floor. This wonderful couple continued to come over for the next eleven days, at which time great friends from Michigan arrived and stayed here with us until we received a response to the advertisement for help in the local paper on Kauai. Soon we hired a wonderful live-in caregiver who happened to have excellent experience and also physical strength.

From that point on, when Jane was out of bed, she was in the wheelchair. Jane never complained once. In our entire marriage, I can never remember a time, including on our travels, when Jane complained.

16. OUR LAST TRIP TO EUROPE

After Jane's diagnosis of Alzheimer's, we continued life as normal. In April, 2011, I talked with our favorite cruise consultant, Harry Kroll at "Cruise Company" and I asked about a 15-night cruise on the Norwegian Sun, leaving Port Canaveral and ending in Copenhagen. We loved Copenhagen. I made this call two weeks before the cruise was to leave, and it was leaving on April 23, our anniversary. I asked him, "Could we get an inside cabin on that cruise for $1,000 apiece?" He said, "Joe, how does $645 sound, including port charges and taxes? That's only $43 a day, and you're having dinner in a 5-Star restaurant." And I replied, "I think that's great." I knew the ship because we had a taken a sister ship out of Venice the year before, a Norwegian line, and I knew that there are four interior cabins that are suite-size for individuals who have wheelchairs. Jane did not yet need a wheelchair at that time, but we had obtained this inside suite-size cabin the year before and I knew that every ship has special interior cabins near the elevator. He said he was on the telephone with them right at that moment, so I gave him the number of the cabin that we wanted (9108) and he said, "I'll ask them." A minute later he said, "You've got it, and if someone does come in late who has a wheelchair, they will upgrade you to another cabin." We flew to Orlando two days before the ship was to sail. We continued our tradition of having only one carry-on bag apiece, plus Jane had a large purse and I had a camera bag.

We stayed in a motel near Port Canaveral. You can see where the space rockets are located. There we got to know a very nice couple from Ohio who were also going to be sailing on the cruise. The ship sailed in the early evening of April 23 on our 51st wedding anniversary. As we left port, Jane and I sat at a window table and we had a five-course dinner with wine. A wonderful anniversary and we both felt extremely happy that we were together enjoying another beautiful trip.

The trip included visits in Ponta Delgada (Azores), Lisbon (Portugal), Bruges (Belgium), Amsterdam (Netherlands) and ended in Copenhagen. Jane and I had never been to the Azores before, but my brother Howard, an Air Force Strategic Air Command (SAC) Officer, had been there many times as the airport in Ponta Delgada was built by the United States and it was long enough for B51 Bombers to land in an emergency and also as a commercial runway for the island.

So when Jane and I were planning our trans-Atlantic trip from Port Canaveral in Florida with the first stop being Ponta Delgada in the Azores, I called my brother and asked him, "Could we go around the island in one day?" Howard replied, "Joe you can go around the island three times in one day." Another couple along with Jane and I rented a taxi with an excellent driver and first toured Ponta Delgada. Then we visited inland villages and volcanic lakes. Volcanic lakes are so unique. Many of them have two colors in the lake. On one side the water of the lake would be green, and the other side would be blue. Another lake may have yellow and pink. It's like there's a line down the middle of the lake; it seems impossible, and it's amazing. We also visited other small villages and had a wonderful lunch in the town on the opposite side from Ponta Delgada. We visited all of the villages except for the most remote one. When we returned to the ship, I am positive that the four of us saw three times more than any of the other passengers on the ship during our time ashore and our cost was probably one-third less of the tour offered by the ship.

The entire cruise was fantastic! For breakfast and lunch Jane and I both went to the buffet which was on an upper deck. The buffet was tremendous and perfect for Jane and me. We became fast friends with the couple from Ohio who we had met at the motel. We would always take the first sitting for dinner. Her husband would go down early before it opened so we were first in line to be able to sit at one of the most beautiful tables for six by the large windows at the stern of the ship. Then his wife and Jane and I would arrive just before 5:30pm and her husband would tell the waiter the table we wanted and that we would welcome other people to join us. Since the table's location was so desirable we would almost always have a full table.

During dinner Jane would sometimes soil her blouse with food. When we returned to our cabin, she would change and I would wash the blouse. Then I would place it in towels (of which the cabin had many) and roll the towels and step on them to absorb the moisture. Then I would hang it up and the blouse would be ready to wear two days later.

Our next stop on the cruise was Lisbon in Portugal. By that time Jane and I had made friends with three sisters on the ship and their husbands. We asked them if they would like to go with us in a nine-passenger van with an experienced driver to see so much more on our tour and at a much lower price than ship-sponsored tours. From Lisbon forward, I would be one of the first passengers to get off the ship to look for a nine-passenger van and talk with the driver and tell him that I wanted as great a tour as he could possibly give us. I went up to the driver who had a nine-passenger van and I told him what we wanted to see and he said, "Great!"

As a result, the eight of us had a fantastic tour. First, we saw all of the sights of Lisbon and then we went to inland villages after which we went approximately 50 miles up the coast. Then we came down along the ocean where there were miles and miles of sand dunes and a few very upscale restaurants. Our driver explained that's where you go for an anniversary party, as they are very expensive. Otherwise there were no homes and the ocean was beautiful. We saw a total of eight surfers out on the water, all wearing wet suits. I asked, "What is the temperature of the water?" It was early June and he said the temperature was 55 degrees. I asked him, "What does it get up to in July or August?" He said it gets up to about 58 degrees. Obviously they were not getting any benefit from the Gulf stream. On the way down the coast, just before reaching Lisbon, we went through this beautiful small town that looked very much like La Jolla and then we returned to our ship.

Our next stop was Bruges where Jane and I had visited numerous times. It was once the royal capital of Belgium (now the capital is Brussels) and it is a very historic and beautiful city. Port Bruges is about four miles from the town of Bruges and that is where we landed. From there we took a van into town, a ten-minute trip and we explored Bruges on our own, including taking a canal tour. Bruges is a beautiful city with a number of canals and a river that connects with the sea.

Our next port was Amsterdam. Jane and I were familiar with Amsterdam and we wanted the other couples to experience the beauty of the area. When I got off the ship, I found this beautiful brand new nine-passenger van, almost as if it was waiting for us. The driver was "Amsterdam Bill." I told him that we wanted to see the city of Amsterdam, and that we wanted to go west toward the North Sea, as far west as the beautiful town of Sneek, Friesland. He said, "That will be perfect. I will take you to a number of villages including my own village and some of the villages on the lake itself. We will stop for lunch in Sneek." We came back on the opposite side of the lake and we got back to our ship just in time to board. When I thanked him, Amsterdam Bill said to me, "Joe, this is exactly why I bought this nine-passenger van three months ago. Yours is the first group that has asked me to do what I was hoping to do, and I thank you very much."

On the last night of the cruise, our Cabin Attendant knocked on our door. He said to me, "I want you to know that among the crew you are the most popular passenger on the ship. We are all so impressed by the loving care you give to your wife." Very kind of him.

Our last stop on the voyage was the beautiful city of Copenhagen. In Copenhagen we knew the area very well, as we had been there a number of times before. That was basically the end of the cruise. Hotel Maritime, located only two blocks away from the famous Nyhavn Harbor (new in the

1700s), is our favorite, relatively inexpensive hotel in Copenhagen. We stayed there for three days and we enjoyed seeing the sights of Copenhagen once again. Among other things we enjoy taking a canal ride and we enjoy walking to the Palace. Jane and I both realized that this would be our last trip to Europe and it was nice to end it in a city we loved. The people are very friendly and we have one favorite restaurant that has a dinner special each night at a very reasonable price. Finding a reasonably-priced restaurant in Copenhagen is an accomplishment, as it is a rare find.

When we are in Europe we almost always fly to Boston from our final destination. We know the least expensive and most wonderful airlines with which to fly, ones not thought of by most Americans. Our flight cost from Copenhagen to Boston, with all airlines except for Iceland Air, would range between $1,175 to $1,250 per person. Luckily we are familiar with Iceland Air and their cost from Copenhagen to Boston, with a stop in the capital of Iceland, Reykjavik, is $650 per person. Their planes are new and the flight attendant staff is outstanding.

Our routine upon returning from Europe over the years was to drive to Newport from Boston and spend five or six days there, because we love it. Also, many of Jane's childhood friends still live there, so we would visit them and take them out for lunch or dinner. Each day we were there, we would take the Ocean Drive. If her friends had not driven the Ocean Drive recently, we would always take them with us.

This time, after landing in Boston, we drove down to our beloved Newport as usual, and I realized that for Jane and me, it could be our last visit there together. Every day that Jane and I were in Newport – from the time we were dating to this final time – we would always take the Ocean Drive. It was sort of a tradition for us. Even when Jane passed away, I made arrangements with the Funeral Director to take the hearse around the Ocean Drive once again.

Being back on Kauai, even though both Jane and I realized that this 2011 trip to Europe would be our last, we continued to feel extremely happy being together. We accepted that we no longer needed the adventure of travel. We simply needed for the two of us to be together. Alzheimer's is progressive and at many points Jane did not know who I was.

17. THE MEMORIAL MASS

Jane died on Thursday, June 19, 2014. There was so much for me to do to get things ready for the flight of Jane's body to Boston, such as picking out Jane's most favorite clothes to give to the wonderful mortuary attendants. I was also coordinating with our children for flight arrangements for us to meet in Boston, and following up with the mortuary in Taunton, Massachusetts, where Jane's mother and father are buried in the Scanlon family plot and where thankfully Jane could also be buried. Also I wanted to arrange for a two-hour detour with the hearse to go once again around the Newport Coastal Drive – even if it was in the dark.

When we left on Tuesday, I was on the same Delta flight as Jane's body and the flight staff were so very kind to tell me – at each stop and take-off – that Jane's body was safely on board.

During those five days between Jane's death and landing in Boston, I had a total of about six or seven hours of sleep – usually in short bites such as a half hour or so. In the Navy I learned how dangerous it is to go more than 72 hours without sleep and we always tried to never exceed 48 hours. While hearing is the last sense to go as the brain is closing down, color is the first thing to go due to sleep deprivation. It is like driving a car and you see that you are low in fuel, you turn off the air conditioner first. Well, by the time we landed in Boston I had lost all sense of color. Everything was black and white. Not a good sign.

But I wanted to complete this last drive of the two of us together and we did drive down to Newport – I was riding in the hearse with the owner of the mortuary, followed by Linda, Mike and Joe Jr. in the car Joe had rented – and we completed the Ocean Drive. The wonderful owner of the Taunton Mortuary then drove to Taunton, and Linda, Joe, Mike and I drove to a motel. Once in bed I fell asleep in seconds and I was able to see color again the next morning.

The family Scanlon plot is in Taunton, Massachusetts and the mortuary is located in a very large and very beautiful colonial house. On Wednesday morning we drove from the motel to Taunton and again met and talked with the owner of the mortuary. He is – as is the cemetery staff – outstanding and we went over the details of the burial and the Catholic service. Jane is buried – thanks to the outstanding cemetery Superintendent and his outstanding Secretary (as described earlier) – right next to her mother and father in a plot that did not exist until the Superintendent said, "Okay, we will make a special exception that we have never made before."

How very helpful and wonderful they both were and I will thank them forever.

On Thursday we were allowed to spend time with Jane's body and she looked so very beautiful. A very wonderful and thoughtful friend had ordered beautiful flowers and those were placed on a table nearest the head of her casket. We each spent time with her alone and prayed for her and we also spent time with her as a family.

On Friday the burial took place at St. Francis Cemetery and we each felt so glad that Jane was buried exactly where she wanted to be, right next to her mother and her father. The flowers that this special friend had sent were placed right at the front of the burial site. A Catholic Burial service was held and we then returned to our motel.

On Saturday some of Jane's nieces and her nephew drove up from Long Island and we went back to Jane's grave site and we all placed a lot of flowers on the grave and we prayed for her. We then went to a very nice restaurant in Taunton and enjoyed getting to know each other better. We discovered how wonderful these relatives we have are.

When we each returned to our separate homes, I immediately started on planning the Memorial service for Jane which would take place in four weeks. I discovered that there is a lot involved in such planning. The service would be held at All Hallows Church in La Jolla where we had been members for forty years – from 1970 to 2010 when we moved to Princeville on the Hawaiian Island of Kauai – and where Jane had been the Hospitality chair person for a number of years. The Pastor at All Hallows is Reverend Father Jerry O'Donnell and he is not only an outstanding pastor, he is also a wonderful, treasured friend. The members of the entire staff are also outstanding and they were all so very helpful.

During this four-week period preparing for the Memorial Mass, I did not feel so terribly sad, as I was determined, working with Father Jerry and the staff, to let everyone know how very special and wonderful Jane was, and I wanted to have a perfect Memorial Service and a very nice reception afterwards. The service and reception went perfectly and so many friends and relatives were there. Father Jerry's Homily for Jane was so very moving and it was perfect.

In his Homily, Father Jerry noted that Joseph Jr. had shared this lovely memory of his mother: "Mom was always reaching out to others and offering her help and friendship. When we first moved to La Jolla,

I remember Mom being surprised that the neighbors didn't rush over to meet us, so she took us to meet them, knocking on everyone's door and introducing us to our new neighbors. Whether it was taking us around to meet neighbors, or helping out with coffee and donuts after Mass, Mom was always reaching out to help others feel at home."

Father Jerry also noted in his Homily: "One of my most vivid memories of Jane dates back to my first time here at All Hollows, as the Associate Pastor, in 1976. Jane and Joe invited me to their home for a party at 6875 Via Valverde. I was a smoker at the time, which seemed like such worldly, sophisticated thing to be doing. I politely asked Jane if it was all right for me to smoke in her house. She said 'No!' but added that if I really had to smoke, I could go outside! That was the very first time anyone had challenged my habit, which eventually led me to ask myself if smoking was all that important to my enjoyment of life. I determined that it wasn't and soon after the Frisinger party I kicked the habit, so, in a very real sense, Jane Frisinger saved my life."

The closing portion of Father Jerry's Homily is so very wonderful.

"The 5th chapter of St. Mark's Gospel tells what I consider to be one of the most poignant and beautiful of all the healing stories of Jesus' ministry. It is the account of how Jesus RESTORED LIFE to the daughter of Jairus! --- Mark says that when Jesus arrived at Jairus' house, he was told that the girl was dead. But Jesus said simply, "Do not be afraid, just have faith." And then, entering the girl's room, Jesus took her by the hand and said to her, "Talitha Koum" which means, "Little girl, I say to you, arise!" And, immediately, the child arose!

"I BELIEVE that this Gospel story became a REALITY in Jane Frisinger's room, in the early evening of June 19th. I BELIEVE that Jesus Christ, the Risen Lord of Life, came to Jane's bedside, at her home on Aloali'i Drive in Princeville, and clasped her by the hand, and said to her, "Talitha Koum" – "Little girl" (because aren't we all the children of God?) – "Little girl, I say to you ARISE!" – "Be free from the earthly shackles of your failing body and mind – be free from your pain and forgetfulness! ARISE, and come with me to My Father's House where you will dwell with all those you have loved, FOREVER – where there will be NO MORE tears – no more suffering – no more LOST MEMORIES – no more sorrow – ONLY JOY!

"And THAT is WHY there can be JOY today, even in the midst of our sorrow. For we have gathered in FAITH – FAITH in the PERSON and in the PROMISE OF JESUS CHRIST who has assured us that even if we've become too feeble for the ordinary tasks of daily life (as Jane was, near the end); even if we can't remember all the "stuff" that was so important to us at ages 20 or 50 or 80 ... even if we can't remember one another – GOD WILL NEVER FORGET US! – And God will one day call

each of US by name – into the GREAT REMEMBERING of ETERNITY!"

After the Memorial Service I suddenly felt lost and extremely sad. I thought there is nothing more I can do for Jane and I miss her so very much. That feeling has continued.

I still have company over once or twice a week and I am often invited to dinner parties arranged by my neighbors. I continue to enjoy going out in the six-person canoes every Monday and Friday mornings. I also am a volunteer at the historic Kilauea Lighthouse (the northern-most Lighthouse in Hawaii) two afternoons a week. I greet visitors and ask if they would like to have their picture taken beside the Lighthouse with their own camera or cell phone and almost everyone says, "Yes, that would be wonderful." So that is a joy for me. But 90% of the time I am alone and my feelings of sadness and longing to be with Jane have never gone away.

Even though I have wonderful caring friends and live in beautiful Kauai, it can be seen as nothing without Jane. Our love was truly perfect, and trusting there is a heaven, it will once again be perfect for Jane and me to be together forever.

18. MY THREE SADDEST DAYS

My saddest day was the day Jane passed away, June 19, 2014. On that particular day, Jane's condition seemed to be stable but I sensed something was wrong. Things just did not seem right to me.

That evening when we were helping Jane get into bed, she seemed to be tense, and I adjusted her pillow thinking it might be that. I gave her a good night kiss and told her, "I love you." Our wonderful young caregiver, like a granddaughter to both Jane and me, gave Jane a kiss, and as I stepped out of the room, the caregiver called, "Joe!" I came back into the room. Jane had just had a massive seizure. Her heart had stopped but her breathing continued, in a gasping-for-breath way. The caregiver immediately began CPR, and I called 911.

Then I kept telling Jane over and over how I loved her, because I know the hearing is the last sense that goes. So she heard that message many times. Her gasping for breath stopped and the CPR did not re-start her heart. Jane had died. The Fire Department arrived and they examined Jane and confirmed that Jane was dead. They asked if she was under hospice care, and I said, "No." They then asked for her doctor's name. They called the emergency number for the doctor and the doctor stated that yes, the death was expected and that she had advanced Alzheimer's Disease and it was a natural death.

Two police officers had also arrived in the meantime and I called the mortuary, as I had already selected the mortuary we would use and I had their phone number. I explained the situation, and the person said that they would send out a van to pick up the body. The Fire Department staff left and the two young police officers said they wanted to stay with us until the body would be taken, "Just to be with you." They were wonderful.

Our neighbors were so very supportive and they were here too. The police were kind in staying with me and with Jane's body until the mortuary attendant arrived. When the van arrived, Jane's body was taken and the police officers and our neighbors left. That was the saddest day of my life.

My second saddest day was when Jane was sitting next to me in her wheelchair and we were watching television. Jane looked at me with fire in her eyes and I had never seen that before. Medically, it's a sign of extreme terror. The fire was right in her eyes and she asked, "Do I know you?" What she was saying was, "I don't know who I am. Do I know you?" I immediately knelt down in front of her and held her hands and told her about her entire life, where she was born, where she grew up, her friends growing up, working for the telephone company, our marriage, our children, our travels. I spent a whole hour. I also took one of the books that she had made for the children and went through that book with her. At the end of that hour, Jane seemed to be relaxed and her eyes were back to normal. She seemed to be at peace.

My third saddest day was a Saturday in September 2015 when all of a sudden I felt that Jane, who had died, was as horribly sad as I was. And I just felt terrible. I thought, if she's as sad as I am, that would be such a horrible thing, because I felt that I was causing her to be sad. The next day, Sunday, at church the regular usher was out of town so I was the usher. I had already been assigned as one of the Eucharistic ministers that day.

As people were coming in, this wonderful woman asked me, "Do you have gluten-free host?" And I said, "Yes, we do, and I will go back and make sure you have it. It will be in a small gold case. I will point you out to the person coming back with the gluten-free host and he will give you that." I asked for her name, and she replied, "Janet." After she received the host, she came to me and I said, "Janet, receive the blood of Christ." It was sheer chance that I was the usher that day as well as being assigned as one of the Eucharistic ministers.

As people were leaving Mass, I was passing out bulletins and when Janet walked by, I asked, "May I talk with you after?" And she said, "Yes." After Mass I asked where she was staying and it was nearby at the Westin, a five-minute walk away across the golf course from my home. I asked, "Could you come over for wine and cheese this afternoon?" And she said, "Yes." When she came over, I learned that Janet was a staff member of the Catholic Diocese of Santa Cruz and she had just left that position to accept a position with Loyola Press, a position that still allowed her to live at her home in Santa Cruz except for initial training in Chicago and periodic returns to Chicago. She was to start that new job in a week.

While we were talking I described how horrible I had been feeling the day before, on Saturday, when I had suddenly thought that Jane was feeling my extreme sadness and that it made her feel terrible and sad too. It seemed to me to be my fault that she was feeling that way, causing her pain, which made me feel even sadder. Janet then told me that at one time she (Janet) was clinically dead and during those few minutes while they were still working on her body, trying to save her life, she felt this enormous feeling of love, all worries were gone, it was a huge light filled with love and she was entering this light, and she was so very happy. As it turned out, they were able to bring her back, but the experience was profound and stayed with her. She said, "Joe don't worry, Jane is feeling nothing but love, so don't worry about it."

As we continued to talk, I asked her, "When is your birthday?" She said, "My birthday is April 13." I said, "What a coincidence, Jane's birthday is March 13 and my mother's birthday is May 13." Then Janet said, "And what day did we meet?" We said together, "On the 13th." Janet went on to say, "I really don't know why I came to Kauai. I had no idea. I had this week off, and I wondered, why am I going to Kauai? I'm going to just be sitting by the pool or in my room. And now I know why I came."

From that moment on, we spent each day together. She stayed over at the Westin nearby each night, and each day we would explore the Island of Kauai. That included taking a helicopter tour of the island on a rainy day, and visiting many of the sights on the island. We went to Brenneke's for lunch on the South Shore, and she took a swim in the Brenneke Beach cove area. What a wonderful gift for both of us, especially for me at a time when I was at the deepest part of sadness and really needed the reassurance. I think that was my Guardian Angel again.

Even though the day before had been my third saddest day, the day that Janet appeared in my life turned out to be probably the happiest day and week since Jane had passed away, because of her assurances that Jane was fine and well. When Janet told me of her near-death experience, I said to her, "I've heard of these stories before, of people describing their near-death experiences, and I would say to myself, 'well, maybe' but hearing it from you, I'm sure it's true, and I'm so glad that you have told me that."

The unusual coincidences of the four dates of 13 added up to make it all seem more genuine to me.

19. BARGAINING WITH GOD

In talking with my wonderful sister-in-law, I said to her, "I've told God that I want to be with Jane and if I'm not with Jane I don't want to be anywhere."

My sister-in-law questioned, "You're bargaining with God?" And I replied, "Yes, I'm bargaining with God. People tell me 'in heaven you're going to be with so many nice people and you will have an overwhelming feeling of love.' I already have that on earth, I have wonderful friends and neighbors, but when I'm alone I feel absolutely horrible and I've made it very clear to God that I would rather be no place and not exist unless I'm with Jane."

And I really feel that way. Jane and I were always so close.

Toward the end of one day when I was going to the canoe club to go out in the six-person canoes, Jane almost pleaded with me, "Can I go with you?" And I replied, "Jane, you've gone down with me twice before. The first time you were sitting in the area that is under the raised club house and you had several insect bites while sitting there waiting an hour and a half for me to come back and no one else was there. On the second time, you were sitting in the car alone for the whole one and a half hours and you were praying that I'd be all right."

At that point in Jane's Alzheimer's Disease we had a live-in caregiver. During the course of her final two and a half years of life, we had three wonderful and talented caregivers who provided loving support to Jane. So Jane was not alone at home when she pleaded, "Can I go with you?"

And I felt so terrible in saying no and explaining why, but I still felt so terrible because she was pleading so desperately and so sadly.

Our son, Joe Jr. visited us when Jane was suffering from Alzheimer's Disease and during one of those visits the three of us drove into Lihue to go shopping. While I went in to a store, he would remain in the car with Jane. On the way back from Lihue we stopped at Safeway for just a few minutes. I wasn't gone more than ten minutes but when I got back into the car my son said, "Jane was so worried about you and kept asking, 'Is Joe all right?' while you were gone."

So we were in a position in which we never wanted to be separated, ever, and certainly I would never want to be separated from her after my death. I would want to be with her, or nowhere.

20. LOOKING BACK

I am telling this story in the summer of 2016, after more than two years since Jane's death. They say that the first year after a spouse's death is the hardest and then things gradually get better. That is not how it is working out for me. I am actually feeling slightly worse each month instead of better. I miss Jane so very much and I also feel lost without her. To the outside world, when I am with others I appear as one of the happiest individuals on earth – greeting people, helping people, remembering names of others and trying to be friends with everyone. I truly feel better if I can be friendly or helpful to others.

During Jane's decline with Alzheimer's, we would have friends (neighbors, church friends, canoe club friends) over for wine and cheese at least twice a week in order for Jane to have contact with others. In one pre-Christmas season a group of neighbors came over to sing Christmas Carols to Jane.

Jane and I had long said that if we were dying together – such as in a plane crash – we would actually be happy as we would be together and we would be holding hands and would be telling each other "I love you." We also felt that if one of us were to die first, we would hope the other would be near us and we knew that if they were near us they would say "I love you" over and over again and hold our hands, as I had done in Jane's final moments.

As it turned out, Jane had a violent seizure, her heart stopped and she was gasping for breath. I knew the last sense to go is hearing, so after I called 911 and while our live-in caregiver was doing CPR on her, I was telling Jane over and over again, "I love you!"

As Jane's Alzheimer's Disease progressed, Jane and I would often say to each other, "I want to be with you forever." Toward to the end of Jane's life, it became a plea from each of us, "I want to be with you forever."

April 23, 1960

My Bride ~ Jane Elizabeth Frisinger

June 19, 2016

My Dearest Wonderful Jane,

Jane, I am so in love with you and I miss you so very much. I want to be with you and I want to be with you forever. Jane, thanks to my Guardian Angel I meet you and I immediately knew that you were the person I love and I was just waiting to see you

Jane you gave me so much confidence that I felt that I could do anything. Without you my confidence level is close to zero. I feel totally lost. You gave me strength, you gave me support and you gave me unconditional love. You were also the smart one that took care of all of our money accounts and you were the "saver" that made our many trips to Europe (and Ireland) possible and made the purchase of our three beautiful homes possible. You have been my dream come true. Jane, my wish is when I die I will meet you and you will say "Welcome Home" and we will be together forever.

I will put this letter in an envelope addressed to Jane Elizabeth Scanlon Fusinger in Heaven.

All My Love,
your Joe

P.S. I am so very proud of you.

111

Letter from Heaven

When tomorrow starts without me
and I'm not here to see
if the sun should rise and find your eyes
filled with tears for me.

I wish so much you wouldn't cry
the way you did today
while thinking of the many things
 we didn't get to say.

I know how much you love me
as much as I love you.
And each time you think of me
I know you will miss me too.

When tomorrow starts without me
don't think we're far apart.
For every time you think of me
I am right there in your heart.

by Michelle Russell

February 14, 2000

My Dearest Jane,
Across the years I will walk with you
in deep green forests; on shores of
sand:
and when our time on earth is through
in heaven, too, I will hold your hand.

I love you with all my heart.
                    Your Joe

A friend asked me to complete this survey.

MARRIAGE LONG-TERM COMMITTED RELATIONSHIP SURVEY

What have been the 5 strengths of your marriage or long-term relationship?

1. Unconditional love for each other.
2. Fidelity.
3. The desire to always want to be with each other.
4. Total and complete trust in the other.
5. Respect and pride for each other.
   Plus I added another:
6. Protect each other and always honor the other's feelings.

Identify 5 stumbling blocks you need to work at in your marriage or long-term committed relationship.
In our 54 years of marriage there was an initial adjustment period of about 4 or 5 months, but there was not a single stumbling block to our marriage. During our 54 years of marriage there was never a single harsh word said to the other and we never – ever – had an argument.

What are some of the ways your relationship has been tested?
Children can sometimes be challenging and test a relationship (weaken or strengthen). In our case, it even strengthened our relationship and the bond we had for each other. Illness, such as Alzheimer's, can really test the strength of a relationship and in our case it even made the relationship stronger. We realized even more our love for and our dependence on the other.

How do you resolve the differences in your marriage or long-term relationship?
With respecting the views and the needs of the other person.

Do you believe a marriage or long-term relationship can be irrevocably broken? If so, what factors might cause a long-term committed relationship to be irrevocably broken?

1. Domestic violence.
2. Infidelity.
3. Major differences in how money should be spent.

Dear Friends,

I wish that I could provide you with a formula for achieving a "perfect marriage" but I cannot. There is no simple formula. It is something that both husband and wife have to work out together as equals and try to make the other's needs their own.

In the case of Jane and me our love for the other and our need for the other increased in intensity throughout our entire marriage – even to the last day of Jane's life. We each realized the great need we had for the other and we could not imagine life without the other. We both knew that we wanted to be with the other forever.

There is, perhaps, one secret toward achieving a perfect marriage and that is recognizing the positive strengths of the other. In a perfect marriage you willingly and gratefully yield to the other. For example, Jane had the strength of being an outstanding money manager, so she managed all of our finances and she did a superb job. Our strengths combined for us to share a wonderful quality of life together.

As with many things in life there is sometimes a downside to what we value as great. Jane and I both hoped that, when we died, we would die together. That did not happen. As the survivor, I feel completely lost and, when I am alone (which is most of the time) I often feel extremely sad. So I deeply appreciate, and am much happier, when visitors stay with me. I also enjoy having people over for wine and cheese, or dinner. Continuing to live, I want to help others as Jane would expect me to do. In the meantime, I do await, perhaps somewhat impatiently, my death and being with Jane forever.

Wishing you a wonderful marriage.

Kindest Regards,

Joe

This book – *A PERFECT LOVE and A BLESSED LIFE* – was first published in August, 2016 and continues to be available for purchase on www.amazon.com.

Contact information:

As Told by:

Joe Frisinger
3962 Aloalii Drive
Princeville, HI 96722
United States
1-808-826-0256
jfrisi2747@aol.com

As Written by:

Lynn Thompson
2-2164 Blossom Drive
Ottawa, ON KIH 6G8
Canada
1-613-799-0323
livingonpurposelynn@gmail.com

Made in the USA
San Bernardino, CA
24 August 2016